BECOMING THE MOTOR CITY

A TIMELINE OF DETROIT'S AUTO INDUSTRY

wherever you go... GO PONTIAC

RELIABILITY ASSURANC
CAR QUALITY AUDIT

PONTIAC

1964 PONTIAC ASSEMBLY LINE
INSPECTION STATION

BECOMING THE MOTOR CITY

A TIMELINE OF DETROIT'S AUTO INDUSTRY

BY **PAUL VACHON**

REEDY PRESS

Copyright © 2021 by Reedy Press, LLC

Reedy Press

PO Box 5131

St. Louis, MO 63139, USA

www.reedypress.com

Library of Congress Control Number: 2021935144

ISBN: 9781681063232

Cover and interior design: Eric Marquard

Page layout: Linda Eckels

Images: All images are believed to be in the public domain unless otherwise noted.

Cover images (*clockwise from upper right*): Charles King w/ car (*Burton Historical Collection, Detroit Public Library*),

Ford Mach-E Mustang (*Public Domain via Autoblog.org*), 1958 Chevrolet Impala Assembly Line (*Public Domain via dbj.org*),

Henry Ford with the Ten Millionth Model and his original Quadracycle (*Library of Congress*)

Retired Brands logos: Courtesy of brandsoftheworld.com

Printed in the United States of America

21 22 23 24 25   5 4 3 2 1

DEDICATION

To the women and men who put America on wheels: laborers, tradespeople, engineers, designers, and managers. And to their present-day counterparts charting the future of mobility.

CONTENTS

Acknowledgments ix

Preface x

CHAPTER ONE: Early Beginnings—Detroit's Industrial Foundation 1

CHAPTER TWO: The Quest for the "Horseless Carriage" 7

CHAPTER THREE: Arrival of the Pioneers—Curious Paths Taken to Detroit 19

CHAPTER FOUR: The Industry Comes of Age 39

CHAPTER FIVE: Years of Consolidation and Depression 57

CHAPTER SIX: World War II and the Arsenal of Democracy 71

CHAPTER SEVEN: The Postwar Years 83

CHAPTER EIGHT: The Late 20th Century (1960–2000) 101

CHAPTER NINE: The 21st Century 115

EPILOGUE: The Promise of New Forms of Mobility 125

Endnotes 151

Appendix 155

Index 162

UNIROYAL TIRE LOCATED OFF I-94 NEAR
DETROIT METROPOLITAN AIRPORT

ACKNOWLEDGMENTS

WRITING A BOOK is always an exciting, if exhausting, undertaking. And while only my name appears on the cover, bringing this project to fruition required the involvement of many others.

I am most appreciative for the inspiration provided to me by Josh Stevens, owner of Reedy Press. After the success of my first book with Reedy, Josh encouraged me to pursue this project. I'm most grateful for his vote of confidence.

My sincere thanks to Barbara Northcott, production director at Reedy Press. Barbara provided me with invaluable guidance concerning text length, image suitability, and how to best express my creativity.

I also want to thank Nia Hasten, public relations manager at Reedy Press, for working with me to effectively market the book.

Special thanks to Elizabeth Clemens, audiovisual archivist at the Walter P. Reuther Library, Archives of Labor and Urban Affairs, at Wayne State University, for providing expert assistance with selecting and procuring many of the book's archival images.

On a personal note, I want to thank my wife Sheryl, our son Evan, and his girlfriend Ella Ackerman, who have had to listen to me talk about my research for the better part of a year.

Lastly, I want to extend deep gratitude to my circle of fellow writers, who have become not only valued peers but close confidants over the years. Their friendship has enabled me to persevere and grow as a writer. While there are too many to name individually, I want to specifically thank Michele Wojciechowski, Laura Laing, Jennifer Fink, Kelly James, Debbie Abrams Kaplan, Kristine Denholm, Anthony Robins, Alexa Stanard, Stephanie Vozza, Kathy Sena, Wendy Helfenbaum, Marian Calabro, and Patchen Barss.

PREFACE

That's a status symbol to say you're from Detroit.
It implies something. You come from a place where
all of this great music and all these great cars,
and all of these great, cool things (are from).

ANTHONY BOURDAIN, 1956–2018

DETROITERS ARE a lucky lot. Whether due purely to an accident of history or the result of a great constellation of investment capital, natural resources, and raw talent, this corner of southeast Michigan has, for more than a century, been principally responsible for the technology that has had the single greatest impact on the United States and the entire globe. Having a front-row seat to this synergy of modern industrial America, Detroiters have benefited from the consequences of economic prosperity, cultural enrichment, and unvarnished hometown pride.

Local media often run auto-related news as their lead stories. A drive between any two random points within the metro area will likely take the rider past a factory, a research and development facility, or a mammoth office building—home to the HQ of a tier-one supplier or of one of the "Big Three" (although now sometimes referenced as the Detroit Three), the collective name for the major domestic manufacturers.

And despite years spent striving toward economic diversification, the city that put the world on wheels continues to pay a steep price for the privilege. Decades of boom and bust, prosperity and recession, and reinvention have left indelible marks on the region in the form of shuttered factories and high-tech startups. The widely cyclical local economy has made the American Dream ever harder to attain because almost every local job rests, however indirectly, on the world's appetite for cars. In Detroit, almost everyone works for the auto industry, literally or otherwise.

TROIT SHIP BUILDING CO. LIFE RAFTS DEPT. 7-10-12.

Blessings provided to southeast Michigan by the auto industry are both numerous and durable. The meteoric rise of its early decades transformed Detroit from a humble, 19th-century working town to what would eventually become the nation's fourth-largest metropolis. Corporate titans used the resulting wealth to shower the city with cultural largesse. The Detroit Institute of Arts, the Detroit Public Library, and the Detroit Symphony Orchestra (all among the finest institutions of their type in the nation) are but a few examples. Generations later, the community continues to benefit from these contributions.

This book seeks to guide the reader along the complex, even byzantine path taken by Detroit's signature business. It's a history that is astonishingly complex, beginning with the early tinkerings of Ransom Olds, Charles King, and Henry Ford—all of whom gained their inspirations from innovators located elsewhere. As cars and trucks evolved technologically, their role in American life transitioned from that of a luxury for the wealthy to a necessity used by generations of workers, tradespeople, farmers, and leisure travelers.

The massive infrastructure built to sustain the industry became a vital national asset during World War II. Detroit became known as the Arsenal of Democracy and made contributions to the war effort exceeding that of any other US city. After reverting to civilian production in the postwar era, the automobile became responsible for the explosion of the nation's suburbs, causing the hollowing out of the central cities and the furtherance of racial segregation. Today, a critical examination of America's landscape will reveal evidence of this unfortunate legacy.

At present, Detroit's auto industry is mired in a period of deep introspection, as it seeks to rethink and redefine mobility and how it can provide modern transportation solutions effectively and sustainably. Ever-present environmental and economic concerns make reassessment an urgent necessity. And while forecasting the future is difficult, preparing for it is essential.

DETROIT'S INDUSTRIAL FOUNDATIONS
DOWNTOWN DETROIT C. 1900

LIBRARY OF CONGRESS

xi

CHAPTER ONE

EARLY BEGINNINGS—DETROIT'S INDUSTRIAL FOUNDATION

BY THE CIVIL WAR era, Detroit was emerging from its longtime identity of a military outpost and taking on the trappings of an urban environment. In 1865, the city established a police department and a public library. And early on, the city's economy gravitated toward heavy industry.

In 1868, local inventor William Davis patented the first refrigerated railway car. Four years later, Elijah McCoy developed and patented a device to supply locomotive engines with a continuous supply of oil, increasing efficiency. By 1880, Detroit's population had expanded to over 116,000, representing more than 40 distinct nationalities and reflecting an increase from just 45,000 twenty years earlier.

Even from the early date, Detroit's central location in the upper Midwest and its position on an international waterway yielded benefits, which would become ever more apparent as the decades progressed.

When examining the industrial background of late 19th-century Detroit, the luxury of retrospection lays out a clear progression. This period fell within the Second Industrial Revolution, which occurred between 1870 and 1914 and was distinguished by impactful breakthroughs in manufacturing, transportation, communication, and electrification. Taking place concurrently in Western Europe and the United States, the the advances from this era allowed farmers to access distant markets, reduced the time required for transcontinental travel from weeks to days, and enabled almost instantaneous long-distance communication via the telegraph. Increased electrification made manufacturing more efficient.

During the 1890s, Detroit benefited from a highly diversified economy, albeit one tilted toward manufacturing. Thomas Klug quotes *Detroit of Today* in saying,

> It is an admitted fact that the true foundation of a city's prosperity is in its manufacturing industries. A prosperity based exclusively upon a commercial foundation must necessarily be ephemeral.[1]

The world took notice. Immigrants from Eastern and Southern Europe came to Detroit by the thousands between 1870 and 1900, swelling the city's population from 79,603 to 285,704.[2] The newcomers arrived with varying degrees of job skills. By 1890 Detroit was home to hundreds of "metal benders," tradesmen who made their living in the major manufacturing concerns of the day.

Stove manufacturing became dominant during the mid-19th century. As early as the 1860s, companies such as the Detroit Stove Works and the Michigan Stove Company produced thousands of the appliances, the latter marketing their product under the familiar Garland name.[3] A modern-day tribute to the industry was the 25-foot stove erected in 1893 for the World Columbian Exposition in Chicago. After the event, the structure was dismantled, moved to Detroit, and eventually displayed at the Michigan State Fairgrounds. Sadly, the much loved landmark burned in 2011, probably due to a lightning strike.

Following the local introduction in 1864 of the new Bessemer method of steelmaking, Detroit became a center for the production of steel rails for railroads, which led to the manufacturing of railcars. One player was the Detroit Car and Manufacturing Company, begun in 1853 by George B. Russel and purchased in 1871 by George Pullman of the eponymous Pullman cars. Pullman eventually relocated the business to Chicago, but Russel's sons soon formed the Russel Wheel and Foundry Company in Detroit, which produced railroad cars specifically designed for logging operations.[4]

In 1885, Charles Lang Freer and Frank Hecker established the Peninsular Car Company. In 1892, the duo entered into a merger combining their company and the Michigan Car Company with Russell Wheel and the Detroit Car Wheel Company, firmly establishing Detroit as an industry leader. The consolidated workforce numbered more than 9,000 and produced some 100 cars per day.[5]

Shipbuilding also emerged during this period, taking advantage of the city's waterfront location. Around 1850, Campbell, Wolverton and Company began as a ship repair shop at the foot of Orleans Street and eventually expanded into steamship building. After the acquisition of the Detroit Dry Dock Company of Wyandotte, the company began producing marine engines. More consolidations followed, making its successor business, the Detroit Shipbuilding Company, the city's fourth-largest employer by 1900, with more than 1,300 workers.[6]

To support all this manufacturing, an extensive network of support businesses developed. According to historian Douglas Brinkley, "If one walked for two miles down Jefferson Avenue, one would have found redbrick warehouses, lumberyards, wharf-front tenements, and machine shops in a scene of industrial angst straight out of the pages of Charles Dickens."[7] This assemblage also included cafes, cobblers, and purveyors of work clothing to support the ever-growing labor force.

This synergy of investment capital, robust workforce, abundant rail lines, and fortuitous geography proved essential in promoting Detroit as the center of the emerging new industry. Yet while several other cities offered these assets, fate may have ultimately played a role. The creative spark provided by Henry Ford, Charles King, and Ransom Olds, who happened to be native to the area, completed the equation and permanently altered history. [8]

WOODWARD AVENUE IN WINTER C.1900

LIBRARY OF CONGRESS

WORLD COLUMBIAN EXPOSITION, CHICAGO; TRANSPORTATION BUILDING, 1893

CHAPTER TWO

THE QUEST FOR THE "HORSELESS CARRIAGE"

MOST ENGLISH-SPEAKING people have a subtle habit—a tendency to name emerging technologies not directly by their new function, but by using the name of its predecessor with a modifier. Referring to early motor cars as "horseless carriages" is but one example.[1] Contemporary examples include "cordless phone," "wireless headset," or "paperless office."

This tendency can serve as a useful gauge for measuring the impact of a new invention. While the precise origin of the term is unknown, its very adoption (and its occasional use even today) is indicative of the radical change in transportation technology that germinated during the 19th century.

While Detroit emerged as the center of the auto industry, this would not have occurred without contributions from Europe and points elsewhere in the United States.

EARLY METHODS OF PROPULSION

■ *LONG BEFORE THE INVENTION* of the internal combustion engine, innovators theorized about a self-propelled land vehicle. As early as 1478, Leonardo Da Vinci conceived of a three-wheeled wagon that became known as a clockwork car. The vehicle was powered by wound springs that would deliver motion by gradually releasing their tension, just like a traditional spring-wound watch.[2] In 1770, French engineer Nicolas Cugnot constructed the first steam-powered vehicle capable of achieving two miles per hour.

Various other inventors explored steam power, including Americans Nathan Read of Salem and Frank Curtis of Newburyport, Massachusetts. In Britain, Sir Goldsworthy Gurney developed two vehicles powered by steam engines; the most efficient weighed 3,000 pounds and was able to carry six passengers. In 1830, he managed to make a trip as long as 84 miles. But strong public opposition to these new inventions sharing the roads with horses led to their demise.

The late 19th century also saw the development of electric vehicles powered by motors linked to rechargeable lead acid batteries. One of the earliest designers was Thomas Parker of London, England, who produced a prototype in 1896, and soon electric-powered tricycles appeared in European cities. The first American version, by William Morrison of Des Moines, Iowa, appeared in 1890.

Initially, electrics seemed to have advantages over gas-powered vehicles. Instead of using a hand crank start, a simple switch was all that was needed. They were also cleaner and quieter. Range and speed were limited, but because most trips were short and took place in urban areas, these disadvantages mattered little.

These early experiments showed promise in steam and electricity as a means of propulsion, and the appeal of the latter would never completely disappear. But by the late 1890s, most of the pioneers had settled on the gas-powered internal combustion engine (although Henry Ford experimented with alternate fuels based on soybeans). The primary reason is the much higher energy density of gasoline versus steam generated from coal or another combustible. This same property presents itself today as engineers strive to design electric vehicles, especially because gasoline has 13 times the energy density of even the most sophisticated lithium ion batteries.[3] Future technical breakthroughs may alter this equation.

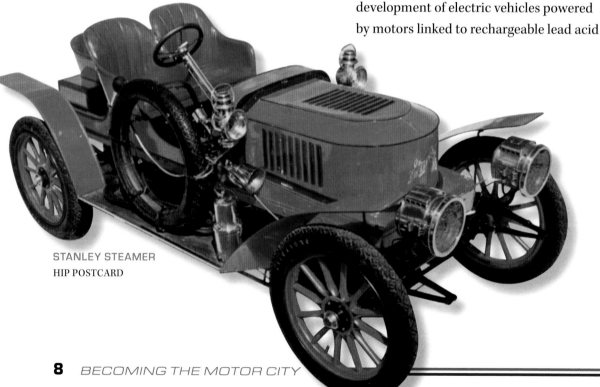

STANLEY STEAMER
HIP POSTCARD

NICOLAUS AUGUST OTTO AND GOTTLIEB DAIMLER

■ **CREDITING ANY INDIVIDUAL** as the "inventor" of the automobile is virtually impossible because the technologies necessary for a working vehicle consisted of a series of breakthroughs conceived (and later refined by) a succession of European inventors. During the mid-19th century, these figures worked concurrently, either in tandem or as competitors.

German engineer Nicolaus August Otto (1832–1891) is a founding member of this group. In May of 1876, after several years of experimentation, he constructed the first four-stroke internal combustion engine. Gottlieb Daimler, Otto's partner at *Deutz-AG-Gasmotorengabrik* in Cologne, wanted to adapt the new machine to a vehicle. Otto had no interest at the time, creating considerable animosity between the two and prompting Daimler to leave.

Daimler later hired a lawyer who discovered that Alphonse Beau de Rochas of France had obtained a patent for a four-cycle engine in 1861, which voided Otto's patent (even though Rochas only sketched out and never built his machine). This opening allowed Daimler to produce copies of Otto's design without paying royalties to his former partner.

Along with his new partner Wilhelm Maybach, Daimler improved on Otto's design, equipping it with a gasoline-injected carburetor and a vertical cylinder. In 1886, the duo adapted a stagecoach to use their engine. The experiment worked, producing what is regarded as the world's first four-wheeled automobile. Their engineering prowess grew, and, in 1890, Daimler and Maybach formed *Daimler Motoren-Gesellschaft.*

KARL BENZ

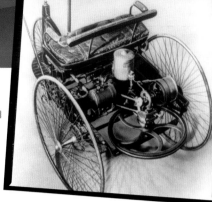

■ **CONCURRENT WITH** Daimler and Maybach's work, engineer Karl Benz of Mannheim, Germany, experimented with a two-stroke engine design. By 1880, he had constructed a reliable prototype and was awarded a patent. His acumen led to his subsequent concepts for other components essential for a motorized vehicle: ignition, spark plug, carburetor, and clutch.

In 1883, Benz partnered with Max Rose and Friedrich Wilhelm Eblinger to form *Benz & Companie Rheinische Gasmotoren-Fabrik* (Benz & Cie). The new company both produced industrial machinery and allowed Benz the opportunity to continue his experiments. In 1885, he unveiled the three-wheeled Benz Patent-Motorwagen, recognized as the world's first production automobile.

The vehicle resembled a giant tricycle with a steel frame and a wood superstructure forming a floorboard and the seat foundation. Under the seat was a 58.2-cubic-inch single-cylinder four-stroke engine. A system of belts served as a one-speed transmission, directing motion to two chain drives. Three spoked bicycle-style tires served as wheels. A tiller mechanism controlled steering, similar to a modern rack-and-pinion system.

Benz subsequently designed improved models of the Motorwagen. In 1888, his wife Bertha drove Motorwagen Number 3 (equipped with brakes, a fuel tank, and a two-horsepower engine) from Mannheim to Pforzheim, a distance of some 60 miles. By doing so, she became the first person to drive a motor vehicle over more than a short distance. While personal in nature, the trip also served as a marketing opportunity. In late 1888, the car became available commercially.

The following years led to more innovation, including Benz's 1896 patent for the first flat engine with pistons horizontally opposed. Simultaneously, additional breakthroughs by Wilhelm Maybach at DMG, including the new Mercedes 35-horsepower engine, led to intensified competition between the two firms. Their 1926 merger formed Daimler Benz AG.

DURYEA BROTHERS

■ **CONCURRENT WITH THE RESEARCH** in Europe, American innovators began to look for improved modes of transportation. In 1886, Charles and Frank Duryea, two brothers from Springfield, Massachusetts, attended a fair in Ohio and observed an internal combustion engine on display. The pair operated a bicycle manufacturing shop, and the sight of the engine stoked their curiosity.

After returning home, however, procrastination took hold. Finally, in 1891, the brothers set out to design a working engine. The result was a one-cylinder, four-horsepower model. Confident in its feasibility, they continued to work on a vehicle. In 1893, they successfully tested their prototype—little more than a buggy with an engine (a literal "horseless carriage").

Improved versions soon followed. In November of 1895, the brothers competed in a 54-mile round trip race between Chicago and Evanston, Illinois. The Duryea's car finished in first place, clocking an average speed of about seven mph and winning the $2,000 prize.

Capitalizing on the welcome publicity, Charles and Frank began the Duryea Motor Wagon Company to produce and sell their car. By the end of 1896, they had sold 13 copies of their vehicle. After five years of operation, the company dissolved due to disagreements between the founders, which included a dispute about moving the company to Detroit.

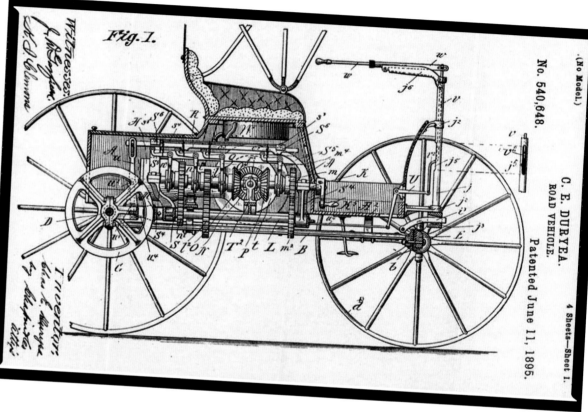

PATENT DRAWING OF EARLY
DURYEA CAR, C. 1895
LIBRARY OF CONGRESS

Both brothers went on to other ventures. Frank partnered with firearm manufacturer Joshua Stevens to form Stevens-Duryea in Chicopee Falls, Massachusetts, which produced various products—including one of the first limousines—until 1927. Charles moved to Reading, Pennsylvania, and began the Duryea Power Company, which built the Duryea Straight-Line Phaeton.

RANSOM OLDS

■ *A CONTEMPORARY OF HENRY FORD,* Ransom Eli Olds shared an essential belief with his rival from Dearborn. When asked on his 80th birthday why he worked to develop the automobile, he replied, "because I didn't like the smell of horses on the farm."[4] Born in Geneva, Ohio, in 1864, Olds spent part of his youth on a farm before the family moved to Lansing, Michigan, in 1880. His father, Pliny Olds, worked as a blacksmith and metalworker, which undoubtedly fostered his son's interest in machines. Once in Lansing, Pliny Olds began a partnership with his older son Wallace to build and repair engines. In 1885, Ransom purchased Wallace's interest in the business and began to produce steam engines, a trade that proved quite lucrative for several years. By 1892, when Olds was seriously researching a moving vehicle, his development of a gasoline-powered steam engine was the subject of an article in *Scientific American,* a prestigious publication with a circulation of more than 50,000. Soon after, Olds mated the engine to a vehicle.

Publicity from the article prompted a company in England to make an offer to purchase the Olds steamer for $400, and, in 1893, Olds shipped the car to the company's office in Bombay, India.[5] But during a visit later that year to the World Columbian Exposition, Olds took note of the large number of gasoline engines on display and decided to move in that direction.[6]

His next breakthrough occurred in August of 1895 when P. F. Olds and Son filed a patent application for a new "gas or vapor engine."[7] For the next several months, the company produced and successfully sold the engine as a finished product, mainly for marine applications. In 1896, Olds decided to use the machine to power an automobile and entered into a partnership with Clark and Son, a Lansing-based carriage manufacturer. The former was to produce a vehicle body with Olds supplying the engine and transmission.

The car, which featured ball bearings and cushion tires and was equipped with two seats and a five-horsepower engine, saw its first public demonstration on August 11, 1896.[8]

OLDS MOTOR WORKS, LANSING, C. 1905

LIBRARY OF CONGRESS

AUTOMOBILE
DRIVERS SHALL NOT
PASS HERE AT OVER
EIGHT MILES "HORN
BY ORDER O.M.WKs

13

CHARLES KING

■ *AS ICONIC AS* Henry Ford's name is to Detroit auto lore, it was a much more obscure innovator who accomplished perhaps the most remarkable local engineering feat.

Charles Brady King (1868–1957) was a native of Angel Island, California. After studying engineering at Cornell University, he migrated to Detroit to make his fortune, first working as a draftsman for the Michigan Car Company. In 1893, while employed by the Russel Wheel and Foundry Company, King attended the World Columbian Exposition in Chicago to demonstrate brakes for railroad cars. While there, he saw a display of Gottlieb Daimler's latest automotive model. Inspired, he returned to Detroit, determined to design and build his own.

His mastery of engineering principles proved invaluable, and on the evening of March 6, 1896, King first test-drove his car in downtown Detroit, beating Henry Ford by three months. Beginning on St. Antoine Street, he proceeded to Jefferson Avenue, turned right, and continued to Woodward Avenue. After making another right turn, he drove north before stopping at Campus Martius. Ford, who felt both admiration and jealousy toward his rival, followed on bicycle.

King later became chief engineer for Northern Manufacturing Company and eventually established the King Motor Car Company. Both ventures allowed him to exercise his considerable talent. His achievements included designing the first drivetrain, integrating engines and transmissions, and pioneering automotive styling work. A renaissance man in the fullest sense, his interests also included art, architecture, literature, and music.

CHARLES KING WITH FIRST CAR

WALTER P. REUTHER LIBRARY, ARCHIVES OF URBAN
AND LABOR AFFAIRS, WAYNE STATE UNIVERSITY

HENRY FORD

■ **BORN IN WHAT** was then Springwells Township in 1863, Henry Ford was the son of an immigrant father from County Cork in Ireland. After fleeing the potato famine in 1847, William Ford migrated to Michigan to join relatives near Detroit. After arriving in America, the Ford family worked as farmers, the same vocation they had pursued in Ireland.

Compared to his European counterparts, Henry Ford projects a strikingly different image as an auto pioneer. Despite not having an education in engineering, Ford's advantages were his razor-sharp mechanical acumen and a dogged determination to solve any problem he confronted.

As Henry grew up, he found the hard, labor-intensive reality of farm life not to his liking. He did, however, develop a keen interest in anything of a mechanical nature. Whether it was childhood toys or farm equipment, young Henry would spend hours dismantling and diagnosing any perceived malfunction. His mother even allowed him to locate a workbench in the kitchen for repairing a watch or anything else mechanical.

YOUNG HENRY FORD
GETTY IMAGES

His passion for machines of any type proved unquenchable. At 15, Henry quit school and left Dearborn for Detroit, where he worked a series of jobs in small machine shops. Five years later, returning to the family farm, he took a job with Westinghouse that required him to service and repair steam engines. The earnings and expertise he acquired ignited his interest in developing a "farming locomotive"—known today as a tractor—to eliminate much of the backbreaking labor of farm life.[9]

That first effort ended in failure. Although the breakthrough Ford sought would not occur until years later, his pursuit of that goal taught him to focus his efforts toward incrementally improving a prototype of any conceptual device to make it functional. Historian Douglas Brinkley writes,

> The pursuit of that grail, that harmony of concept and mechanics that would result in an efficient, smooth-running "farm locomotive," drove Henry Ford all his life, through every one of his endeavors from fixing watches to maintaining steam engines to building better gas-powered cars to founding the world's first mass-market automobile company. His perfectionism centered on improving the fundamentals of vehicle engineering, boosting power without adding weight, connecting engines to drives and wheels to chassis for optimum performance, and inventing the tools that could produce the mechanical advances he had in mind.[10]

After marrying Clara Bryant in 1888, the couple continued to reside near the family farm before moving to Detroit in 1891. Henry's goal was to acquire the additional knowledge he would need to design and build a horseless carriage. The young inventor took a job with what was then

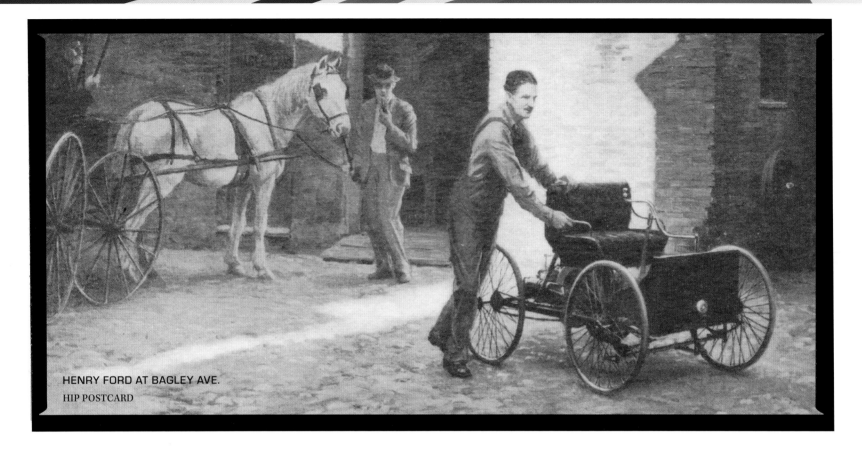

HENRY FORD AT BAGLEY AVE.
HIP POSTCARD

called the Edison Illuminating Company to oversee one of its steam generators that supplied electricity to homes, businesses, and the city's new streetlights. His salary, $90 per month by 1893 (substantial for the time), allowed him to fund his after-hours experiments.

In December 1893, he successfully tested a small gas engine in the couple's kitchen. By 1896, he had completed his first rudimentary car, dubbed the Quadricycle. Cobbled together from angle iron, a leather belt, a chain, four wheels taken from bicycles, and a seat from a buggy, the vehicle's crowning jewel was its two-cylinder, four-horsepower motor, and a three-gallon fuel tank mounted under the seat. It also had a two-speed transmission, but no reverse gear.

On June 4, 1896, Ford unveiled his creation at the workshop behind his home on Bagley Avenue. Intending to take it for a test-drive immediately, Ford then noticed that the building's doorway was too narrow for the car to exit. Ford then took an axe to the brick wall to enlarge the opening to allow the vehicle egress. After several drives, he was able to achieve a speed of 20 mph. Today, the original Quadricycle resides at the Henry Ford Museum of American Innovation in Dearborn.

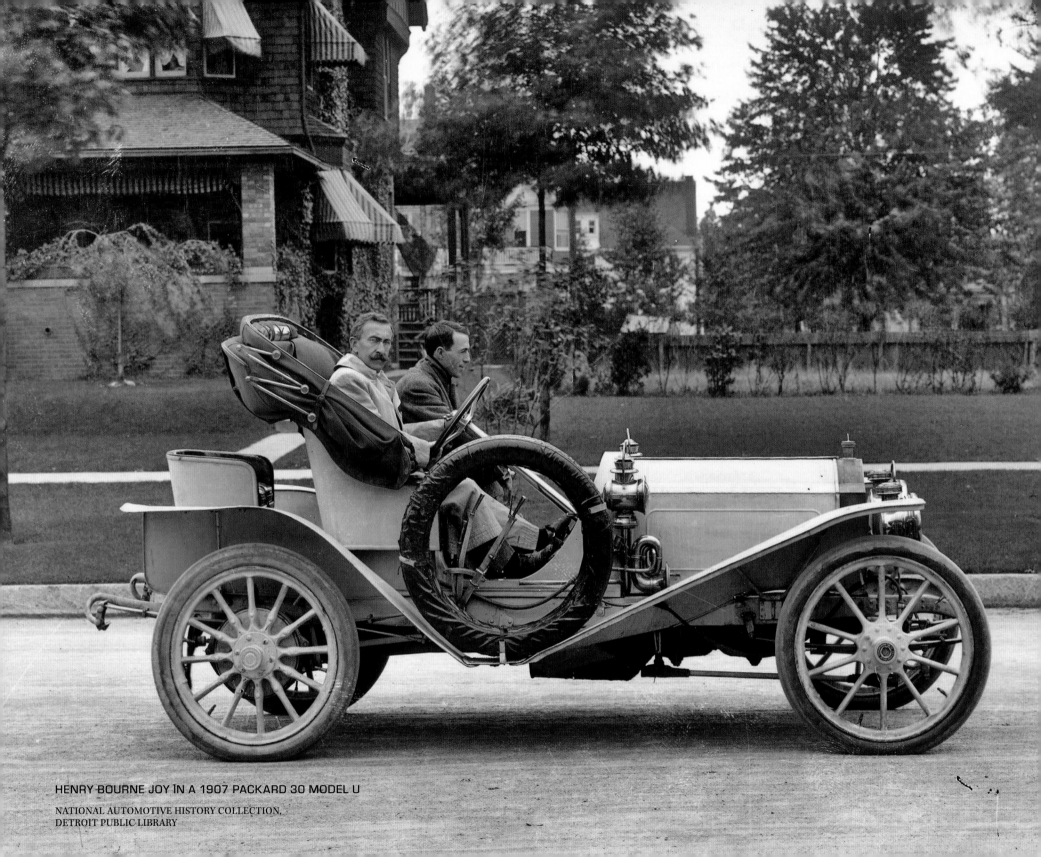

HENRY BOURNE JOY IN A 1907 PACKARD 30 MODEL U

NATIONAL AUTOMOTIVE HISTORY COLLECTION,
DETROIT PUBLIC LIBRARY

CHAPTER THREE

ARRIVAL OF THE PIONEERS—CURIOUS PATHS TAKEN TO DETROIT

DESPITE THE ABUNDANCE of innovation in Michigan, the beginning of the 20th century saw the most significant number of automakers take root in cities to the east. In 1905, New York, Chicago, Cleveland, and Boston all boasted more automotive manufacturers than Detroit.[1]

But during the following five years, auto production began to migrate from several divergent locations to cities in the Midwest, particularly Detroit. Historian G. T. Bloomfield cites poor strategy for the demise of automakers elsewhere:

> Errors of technical and market judgment by early New England companies, such as the concentration by Pope-Hartford (based in Hartford, Connecticut) on electric and steam vehicles, contributed to the decline of the other regions. Over the next five years, Michigan and Detroit confirmed their lead when almost two-fifths of the value of production came from the area. Capital investment in the automobile industry between 1904 and 1909 amounted to $150 million, of which Michigan accounted for more than one third.[2]

OLDS MOTOR WORKS

■ **THE TECHNICAL SOPHISTICATION** of Ransom Olds's first car did not go unnoticed by the media. During his demonstration of the new machine in August of 1896, the engineer put the vehicle under a series of rigorous tests, including hill climbing and shifting from low to high gear, eventually achieving a speed of 18 miles per hour. The *Detroit News* commented, "There is no doubt that the much mooted question of the horseless carriage has been successfully solved by Messrs. Olds & Clark."[3]

The exposure paid off, and orders soon poured into Olds's shop. Olds, however, had severely limited production capabilities. To obtain the needed capital, he recruited outside investors. In August of 1897, the budding automaker incorporated as Olds Motor Vehicle Company. New directors included Lansing businessmen Edward W. Sparrow, Eugene Cooley, Arthur C. Stebbins, and Samuel L. Smith, who authorized an offering of $50,000 in stock. Soon a parallel company, the Olds Gasoline Engine Company, was formed specifically to supply engines. The moves provided Olds with the means to manufacture and market his vehicle, but it resulted in a loss of autonomy.

Although this infusion of capital caused business for the engine company to grow exponentially, vehicle production proceeded slowly. In 1899, the two companies merged, and Smith increased his investment. He subsequently sold a number of his shares to associates in both Lansing and Detroit.

The more diverse ownership set their sights on more robust production, resulting in the decision to move operations to Detroit in 1900 due to the myriad advantages offered in Michigan's largest city. According to historian George May, "the advantages that a city of Detroit's size offered in terms of skilled labor, suppliers, and shipping facilities were certainly important considerations."[4] The company purchased five acres of land off Jefferson Avenue near the bridge to Belle Isle to build plants to assemble components and complete vehicles.

One year after Olds's move to Detroit, the company decided to move away from its original design. Priced at $2,800, the car was inaccessible to all but the wealthiest of consumers. The automaker replaced it with the new curved dash runabout, a vehicle aimed at a mass market and priced at only $600 (later raised to $650). By doing so, the company returned to Ransom Olds's original vision of a simple, practical car—similar to those of Charles King and Henry Ford.

Scarcely had production begun, however, when tragedy struck. On March 9, 1901, a fire engulfed the new plant, destroying all facilities except for the foundry. But the adroit company made a quick comeback. Ransom Olds and Secretary-Treasurer Fred Smith (son of investor Samuel Smith) set up temporary facilities, relied more on outside suppliers for major components, and eventually reactivated the original Olds facility in Lansing. While the fire destroyed blueprints and patterns, a quick thinking employee saved one car (a curved dash runabout) from the flames. Several other prototypes were lost. Engineers were able to dismantle the vehicle and used the parts as templates to replace the drawings.[5]

In the subsequent months and years, however, considerable friction developed between Olds and Smith. Olds had returned to Lansing, and although he was general manager of the company, Smith exercised

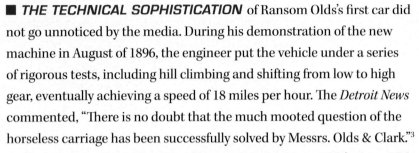

outsized influence at the rebuilt Detroit location. Disagreements over new products, including Smith's desire for a larger touring car, only added to the tension. In 1904, Olds sold his interest and left his namesake company.

The Smiths continued to run Olds Motor Works, changing its focus from the economical runabout to larger, more profitable cars. These changes failed to resonate with the public, and, in 1908, the controlling family accepted William Durant's offer to purchase the company to become part of General Motors (GM).

1901 OLDS CURVED DASH
HIP POSTCARD

HENRY FORD'S FIRST VENTURES

■ **AFTER HENRY FORD'S** successful 1896 test of his first quadricycle, he built an improved version in 1898. In 1899, he constructed yet another machine equipped with brakes, cylinder jackets, and a water tank.[6] Local luminaries, including the mayor of Detroit, William Maybury, soon took notice. Seeing the promise of Ford's work, a group of local businessmen formed the Detroit Automobile Company on August 5, 1899, with Henry Ford as both a director (despite not being required to invest any capital) and an employee. The entity was Detroit's first automaking business. Ford's job was to engineer a line of cars and start a factory to assemble them at a profit.[7]

Joining the new business was a risk for Ford, as it required him to leave his longtime job at the Detroit Illuminating Company. After assembling a team of helpers, Ford rented shop space at a facility on Cass Avenue. In early 1900, the company produced its first vehicle, a truck intended for making deliveries.

While the vehicle was modestly successful, Ford and his team could not achieve cost efficiency by speeding up production, causing the new company to operate at a loss. These difficulties, combined with Ford's lack of personal discipline, led to a falling out with most of his backers. Ultimately, the investors' desire for profitability conflicted with Ford's insistence on technical perfection. In November 1900, the company folded.

But Henry Ford's magnetic personality continued to attract members of the monied class. During the Detroit Automotive Company's brief life, Ford secretly worked on a racing car: a two-cylinder, 2,200-pound behemoth. It had no commercial potential and at the time seemed little more than a vanity project. But in October 1901, Ford entered the car in a 25-mile race at a track in Grosse Pointe Township. After Ford's car managed a surprise win over Cleveland automaker Alexander Winton, his only opponent, some former investors opted to give Ford another chance. The new enterprise was named the Henry Ford Company, with its namesake as its chief engineer. The goal was to produce a reliable, lightweight car for under $1,000.

Unfortunately, Henry Ford failed to learn from his past mistakes. Soon after opening his shop, he spent much of his time designing yet another race car. He dubbed it the 999. The vehicle was nine feet in length and sported a four-cylinder engine. But at the same time, Ford neglected his primary responsibilities. The investors were not pleased and soon showed him the door. Ford departed with rights to his design work and $900 in cash.

Not to be deterred, Ford, who believed the racing circuit held greater potential for reward than producing a car for daily use, completed the 999 with the help of a few benefactors. On October 25, 1902, the car raced in the Manufacturers' Challenge Cup held in Grosse Pointe Township. Driven by Ford's partner Barney Oldfield, the car beat two opponents, finishing the five mile course in 5 minutes and 28 seconds.

And once again, curious investors were watching.

HENRY FORD WITH BARNEY OLDFIELD AND THE 999

WALTER P. REUTHER LIBRARY, ARCHIVES OF URBAN
AND LABOR AFFAIRS, WAYNE STATE UNIVERSITY

CADILLAC AUTOMOBILE COMPANY

■ *BACK AT* the Henry Ford Company, investors Lem Bowen and William Murphy feared the unceremonious departure of its namesake would spell the business's end. They soon enlisted the help of machinist and businessman Henry Leland to appraise the factory and equipment for liquidation purposes.

A former gunsmith who had produced high-quality components for Olds Motor Works, Leland was the consummate professional. He believed in crafting parts of impeccable quality. When Leland arrived, he brought along a one-cylinder engine similar to the one he produced for Olds. After seeing its efficiency and functionality, the investors became receptive to Leland's suggestion to continue the business and build a car using his model engine.

On August 27, 1902, the company was reorganized and renamed the Cadillac Automobile Company in honor of Detroit's founder, Antoine de la Mothe Cadillac. Leland was made a partner in the firm and would be responsible for many future years of success. In 1909, Leland sold Cadillac for $4.5 million to William Durant, who made it the luxury capstone of GM.

Leland stayed with Cadillac until 1917 before leaving over a disagreement with Durant. The US government wanted the company to produce the L-12 Liberty engine for the Army Air Corps. Leland wanted to accept the work, but Durant refused due to his pacifism. Cadillac continued as a luxury carmaker and has proven to be one of the industry's most durable names.

CADILLAC EMPLOYEES

LIBRARY OF CONGRESS

HENRY BOURNE JOY AND PACKARD

■ **IN 1898 JAMES WARD PACKARD** of Warren, Ohio, made what would become a monumental decision. After purchasing one of the first cars built by Winton Motor Carriage Company of Cleveland, he experienced a less-than-pleasant trip back to Warren, as the car broke down several times. After Packard returned to Cleveland to express his displeasure, Alexander Winton angrily responded, "If you're so smart, Mr. Packard, why don't you build a car yourself?"

Packard took up the challenge and set to work with his brother, William Dowd Packard, and designed a one-seat car with tiller steering and a 12-horsepower engine, powerful for its day. The car performed well, leading to new designs that prioritized speed and comfort. Subsequent models set a new standard for luxury, carrying prices as high as $7,500.

In 1902, Henry Bourne Joy of Detroit bought a Packard and was so impressed that he visited Warren and, with his brother-in-law Truman Newberry and Russell Alger Jr., invested $25,000 in the company. He later convinced other Detroit businessmen to kick in $250,000, achieving a controlling interest. After moving the company to Detroit, the new owners commissioned architect Albert Kahn to design a mammoth new factory on East Grand Boulevard.

PACKARD requires in upholstery all that modern science can add to the ancient art of textile weaving. Skilled specialists select the finest fabrics from the looms of Europe and America. Quality first, then beauty of color and design are considered.

From the whole world of materials open to its choice Packard has selected the most beautiful, durable and appropriate broadcloths,

silks and velours. These are immediately available. From them the Packard Eight buyer may choose with the assurance that they represent not only perfect workmanship but exquisite taste.

For those desiring the individuality of custom bodies and special upholstery, Packard quickly procures tapestry, needlepoint—any fabric which the most exacting buyer wishes.

PACKARD

ASK THE MAN WHO OWNS ONE

PACKARD AD C. 1927

PACKARD PLANT
UNDER CONSTRUCTION

LIBRARY OF CONGRESS

JOHN AND HORACE DODGE

■ *ALMOST SIMULTANEOUS* with Olds's arrival, John and Horace Dodge opened their machine shop at Beaubien and Lafayette Streets. Funding their new venture from the sale of their bicycle company in Windsor, Ontario, the pair were no strangers to hard work.

After learning the trade from their father while growing up in Niles, Michigan, John and Horace were inseparable, with John possessing business acumen and Horace the necessary technical knowledge.

In 1901, the Dodge brothers secured a contract with Olds to build 2,000 engines, followed by a deal for 3,000 transmissions the following year.[8] But the brothers soon embarked on a new venture that would produce one of the most significant windfalls in American business.

DODGE MAIN (SKETCH) C. 1919

LIBRARY OF CONGRESS

FORD MOTOR COMPANY

■ **HENRY FORD'S UNLIKELY** 1902 victory in the Manufacturers' Challenge Cup thrust the aspiring automaker back into the limelight—enough to convince coal merchant Alexander Malcomson to back Ford's third automaking effort. Malcolmson was impressed by a design Ford and Harold Wills produced for a vehicle that would become the original Ford Model A. The car offered a two cylinder, eight-horsepower engine and could accommodate two people. It came equipped with two forward gears controlled by a foot pedal.[9]

The duo formed the partnership of Ford and Malcolmson Ltd. to produce and market the car. Due to limited shop capacity, Ford contracted the Dodge Brothers to supply 650 "rigs"—the engine, transmission, axles, and chassis. Before work could begin, Dodge needed to retool its shop at Lafayette and Hastings Streets and invest in raw material, moves that cost some $60,000.[10] But right out of the gate, Ford burned through most of his startup capital, making it impossible to pay his principal supplier. Malcolmson then proposed incorporating the business to attract additional investors. For help, he turned to his uncle John Gray, a local bank president. After much convincing, Gray offered to serve as president, with Henry Ford as the vice president.

The Dodges were asked to contribute to the new venture by forgiving $7,000 in past due balances and investing $3,000 in cash. In return, the brothers collectively received 10% percent of the new company's stock, while John Dodge would serve as vice president. On June 16, 1903, the Ford Motor Company was incorporated.

In addition to the Dodges, Ford, Malcolmson, and Grey, the roster of original investors included John W. Anderson, Horace Rackham, Charles Bennett, Vernon Fry, Albert Strelow, Charles Woodall, and James Couzens, who became Ford's financial secretary. Legend has it that one additional investor wanted to join but was turned away at Henry Ford's insistence, fearful that a 13th party would bring bad luck.

The new undertaking carried considerable risk, prompting the top tier of Detroit's business community to take a pass. The $28,000 cash investment came from 12 less-than-wealthy investors who scraped and borrowed to start the company. If sales lagged, no additional resources would be available.[11]

Ford Motor Company soon opened its first production facility at 588 Mack Avenue (near the present-day intersection with Mt Elliott Avenue). On July 23, the company sold its very first car, a Model A. For Henry Ford, this milestone came none too soon, as the funds fronted by the investors had dwindled to only a few hundred dollars. But success soon followed, and by October, the company realized profits of more than $37,000.

FORD MOTOR COMPANY

DETROIT AUTO PAINTING CO.

THE SELDEN PATENT

■ **NO SOONER** had the new industry found its footing than an exploitation of the patent law threatened its very existence. The issue took root in 1878 when Rochester, New York, patent attorney George Selden, who had a side interest in mechanical devices, designed an internal combustion engine. Selden drew his inspiration from inventor George Brayton's larger version, which he had seen at the Centennial Exhibition of Philadelphia two years earlier. He also sketched out a compatible car.

Although Selden never actually built the vehicle, he decided to file a patent on his design. But after applying, he spent the next several years adding amendments, which roughly corresponded to ongoing developments in the burgeoning industry. His scheme was to use his patent, once issued, to extract royalties from any automaker using "his" design.

Selden carefully worded his application in vague terms so that it would technically apply to gas-powered vehicles built in the Unites States until 1912, its expiration date. After first attempting to fight Selden in court, a group of automakers formed a consortium in 1903 called the Association of Licensed Automobile Manufacturers (ALAM) to collectively negotiate payments with Selden. Begun by Alexander Winton of the Winton Motor Carriage Company of Cleveland, ALAM later included Packard and Olds.

But after striking a deal with Selden, the ALAM functioned as his representative. Only ALAM members were allowed to pay Selden the lower rates, and ALAM only admitted parties it considered "legitimate" automakers—those that manufactured their own parts. This rule effectively froze out Ford Motor Company due to its relationship with Dodge.

The result was a patent infringement lawsuit filed by the ALAM against Ford Motor Company. As the case proceeded, it was Henry Ford who won in the court of public opinion. Seen as the champion of the little guy persecuted by a greedy monopoly, the episode cemented his position as a folk hero. The resulting publicity boosted Ford sales considerably. In a 1909 verdict, Ford lost the case, but he won an appeal in 1911. The ALAM reorganized as a disseminator of industry information but dissolved in 1912. Soon after, its functions were assumed by an organization with a familiar name, the Automobile Association of America, also known as Triple A.[11]

THE FORD MODEL T

■ **FORD CONTINUED** to experience strong demand throughout its first year, necessitating a larger facility. In October, the company moved operations several blocks north to a new, 67,000-square-foot factory at Piquette and Beaubien Streets. Built on a site selected for its proximity to a major railroad junction, the three-story building (10 times larger than the Mack Avenue shop) offered ample space for production, offices, two machine shops, and experimental labs. The neighborhood, known as Milwaukee Junction, later became home to competing automakers, including Anderson Electric, Cadillac, Hupp, and Oakland (later known as Pontiac).

The additional space allowed Ford to expand its product offerings and produce several models simultaneously. Over the next

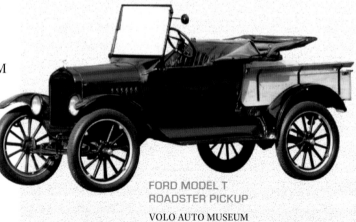

FORD MODEL T
ROADSTER PICKUP

VOLO AUTO MUSEUM

several years, the company introduced an "alphabet soup" of eight new models, including Models B (a more expensive four-cylinder touring car), C, and F (successive improvements over the Model A), plus the K, N, R, and S. Aside from the Model B, each version adhered to Henry Ford's vision of offering a simple, modestly priced car to the mass market.

In early 1907, Ford set up an experimental room on the third floor. Access was strictly limited. During the next several months, Henry Ford, Harold Wills, and Joseph Galamb developed the prototype for what would become the Model T, an entirely new vehicle that became known affectionately as the Tin Lizzie.

The new car proved immediately popular with the public after its October 1908 debut. Sporting a 2.9-liter, four-cylinder engine that produced 20 horsepower, the car was capable of running on kerosene or ethanol in addition to gasoline. Despite the introduction of new features, the car still had a relatively simple design that assured reliability. Its inaugural price was $825 for the runabout version and $850 for the touring car.

Contrary to popular belief, the first Model Ts were not available in black only. In fact, during its first six years, black was not even among the available options. Choices included gray, green, blue, and red, depending on the specific style chosen (touring car, town car, coupe, etc.). In 1914, black became the standard.

From the beginning, production was a laborious, time-consuming process. Each car was constructed by hand on sawhorses. But in 1908, experiments were first conducted at Piquette on a new assembly process: a system where a vehicle would take shape on a moving conveyor.

FORD MODEL T
TOURING EDITION
LIBRARY OF CONGRESS

DODGE BROTHERS MOTOR COMPANY

■ **AFTER TURNING DOWN OTHER BUSINESS** from Olds Motor Works in 1903, Dodge operated for the next 10 years working exclusively for Ford, a relationship that proved quite profitable. For a full decade, the Ford/Dodge relationship existed as a symbiosis, growing and prospering in lockstep. Ford's 1908 introduction of the Model T proved so successful that to meet demand, the deluge of work forced Dodge to build a new, much larger factory in Hamtramck. It was strategically located close to Ford's new Highland Park facility, and the two plants were linked by rail. Through 1914, their dual status as a supplier and part owner of Ford netted the brothers more than $5 million in profits and dividends.

In 1913, the Dodges incorporated their business as the Dodge Brothers Motor Company. The next year, they decided to end their supplier relationship with Ford, fearing the heightened risk of being solely dependent on one customer. The brothers continued, however, as Ford stockholders, appreciative of the lucrative dividends paid. But by the following year, the Dodge brothers would hatch a new project destined to draw the ire of Henry Ford.

In 1919, Henry Ford sought full control over his company and bought back the outside investors' stock. The Dodges sold their 10% stake (acquired from an original investment of only $10,000) for $25 million.

FORD MOVES TO HIGHLAND PARK

■ **HISTORIAN DOUGLAS BRINKLEY** coined the term "Model T Mania" to describe the wave of enthusiasm that overtook the nation after the car's 1908 introduction.[12] Hundreds of Americans relished the sudden improvement to their quality of life brought by on-demand mobility. Besides appointments and personal errands, the car introduced what became a popular American tradition: the automobile vacation.[13]

It soon became apparent that the now cramped Piquette plant was inadequate. Soon Henry Ford commissioned architect Albert Kahn to design a sprawling new factory in what was then the rural community of Highland Park. The result was a complex of modern, efficient buildings on a 12-acre site at Woodward Avenue and Manchester Street. It opened on January 1, 1910.

The new plant featured open, spacious production floors lit by skylight and glass curtain walls. The extra space allowed the optimal placement of machinery and an efficient flow of materials. It was also the first example of Henry Ford's desire for vertical integration; a power plant, foundry, and machine shops were all housed within the campus.

FORD HIGHLAND PARK PLANT—AERIAL VIEW

WALTER P. REUTHER LIBRARY, ARCHIVES OF URBAN AND LABOR AFFAIRS, WAYNE STATE UNIVERSITY

All these assets would be essential when, in 1913, Ford introduced its first assembly line, where a car would progressively take shape while moving along a conveyor. Charles Sorenson, Ford's production chief, described its intricacies when he wrote, "The function of the final, moving assembly line, first tested in 1908 and first installed in 1913, is to put together a number of pieces or parts arriving at that line in an orderly sequence. And those pieces had to be put together before there could be a final assembly."[14] Months of brainstorming and tinkering yielded an optimal level of efficiency.

PRODUCTION LINE AT HIGHLAND PARK

GETTY IMAGES

WILLIAM DURANT TAKES OVER BUICK

■ *BY THE MID-20TH CENTURY,* staid, conservative personalities, such as Henry Leland, Walter Chrysler, and Alfred Sloan, personified the American auto industry. In fact, one could argue that the button-down, analytical approach championed by Sloan came about as a backlash to the flamboyant and overly aggressive style championed by his predecessor.

William C. Durant, a native of Boston, started his business career manufacturing horse-drawn carriages. In 1886, he partnered with J. Dallas Dort and established the Flint Road Cart Company. From this humble beginning, the duo realized remarkable success, gradually forming a series of sister companies and subsidiaries. Much of this growth can be attributed to Durant's "restless, innovative, gambling spirit."[15]

In 1904, William Whiting, an associate of Durant, purchased an interest in the Buick Auto-Vim Company, a Detroit engine company begun by former plumbing entrepreneur David Dunbar Buick. Although the company appeared to have little value, it had recently received a patent for a two-cylinder overhead valve engine (then known as valve-in-head) developed by employee Walter Marr. Whiting soon relocated the company (then named Buick Motor Company) to Flint, with Buick staying on a chief engineer.

David Buick wanted to build the engine for marine applications, while Whiting and Marr advocated a shift toward auto production. But Whiting soon ran short of capital, prompting him to recruit Durant as an investor. This infusion of cash allowed the company to begin producing the Model F. It had a two-cylinder overhead valve engine and an 87-inch wheelbase. By 1908, Buick's production reached some 8,800 cars.[16]

WILLIAM DURANT IN DOORWAY

WALTER P. REUTHER LIBRARY,
ARCHIVES OF URBAN AND LABOR
AFFAIRS, WAYNE STATE UNIVERSITY

1908 BUICK MODEL 10
HIP POSTCARD

MEN MASSED OUTSIDE FORD HIGHLAND PARK PLANT

CHAPTER FOUR

THE INDUSTRY COMES OF AGE

THE SECOND DECADE of the 20th century saw the Detroit auto industry emerge from its infancy. What had just 10 years earlier been an assemblage of workshop tinkerers and gritty mechanics was suddenly transformed into a series of profitable businesses producing a new product embraced enthusiastically by the public. In the process, manufacturers gradually evolved to serve a specific niche, such as luxury cars, delivery trucks, or vehicles for the mass market.

The rate of growth was at times astonishing. Ford Motor Company doubled in size each year, enabling it to purchase one of its major suppliers, the John R. Keim Company, a steel mill in Buffalo, New York.[1] With the acquisition, Ford gained an exceptional employee, William S. Knudsen, whose expertise would be invaluable in the future.

Meanwhile, John and Horace Dodge, using capital gained from their lucrative partnership with Henry Ford, would soon unleash an unwelcome surprise on the self-made mechanic from Dearborn.

THE FORD ASSEMBLY LINE AND THE FIVE-DOLLAR DAY

■ **FORD MOTOR COMPANY'S** Highland Park plant was unlike any other industrial operation. Besides having the best equipment and facilities, the operation placed a high priority on one goal: the constant improvement of its production processes to turn out more cars in less time at the lowest possible cost.

The company's efforts produced a quantum leap in 1914 with the introduction of its first assembly line. Capitalizing on experiments done earlier at the Piquette plant, the concept involved placing staff at stations along a moving conveyor. Each worker performed a strategically ordered task, resulting in a finished product. Initially, lines were set up to produce principal components and subassemblies—crank and camshafts, magnetos, axle assemblies, and so on. Eventually, these lines merged into a final line from which the finished car would emerge.

While the new method was a boon to productivity, the added stress became unbearable for many employees. Intense drudgery and boredom contributed to a depressing life for many a factory worker. Absenteeism and turnover, problematic under the old system, were exacerbated with the introduction of the assembly line. Health and safety issues were frequently ignored by Ford and other employers, creating sympathy for socialism and unionism.[2]

These forces motivated Henry Ford to make an audacious move. On January 5, 1914, Ford Motor Company announced that workers' wages would more than double, from $2.34 per day to $5. Shifts would also be reduced from nine to eight hours. The change immediately reduced absenteeism and improved factory morale. It also achieved the goal of allowing Ford workers to afford to purchase the cars they were building, expanding the company's market base.

However, the higher wages came with strings. Only male employees with a minimum of three years' seniority were eligible. Smoking and drinking (on and off the job) were forbidden, and workers were subject to home visits by members of the company's Social Department, who would check for cleanliness and order. Housewives who were immigrants were even instructed in the proper methods of "American housekeeping."

Despite these restrictions, the $5 per day wage was hugely impactful, both within the company and in society. Under the newly coined moniker of Fordism, the relationship between employer and employee fundamentally changed. The concept of total subservience shifted to a more transactional partnership, where wages were traded for labor. Fordism was also credited with creating the American middle class and, by extension, the consumer-based economy that shaped 20th-century America.

WORKERS LEAVING FORD
HIGHLAND PARK PLANT
LIBRARY OF CONGRESS

DODGE LAUNCHES THE MODEL 30-35 TOURING CAR

■ **ALTHOUGH THEY HAD ENJOYED YEARS** of mutual prosperity, by 1913, the relationship between Henry Ford and the Dodge brothers was starting to fray. John Dodge decided to resign as vice president of Ford Motor Company, and the brothers terminated their role as a supplier to the automaker. Meanwhile, both companies had constructed huge new plants for their own strategic reasons. Ford wanted to begin parts production in-house, while the Dodges aimed to build and market their own car.

In 1914, Dodge introduced the Model 30-35 touring car. The vehicle represented a step forward in auto design, sporting an all-steel frame (as opposed to one made partially of wood), a 12-volt electrical system, and a 35-horsepower engine. These features were seen as improvements over Ford's Model T. Sales were brisk, owing mainly to the Dodges' well-honed reputation for quality. By 1916, variants of the Dodge car collectively ranked number two in sales in the nation.

Not surprisingly, Henry Ford did not take kindly to the development. He resented that the Ford dividends the Dodges received each year (over $1 million) went to developing a competing product. To thwart this perceived disloyalty, Ford moved to drastically reduce dividend payments to all stockholders, partly out of revenge, but also to fund a massive new project. The result would be a lawsuit of legendary proportions.

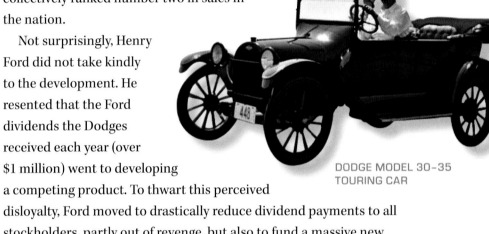

DODGE MODEL 30-35 TOURING CAR

DODGE V. FORD MOTOR COMPANY

■ **BY 1915, HENRY FORD** had developed his personal philosophy of business: continuously increase production to drive down costs and therefore prices. By making a car affordable to more people, sales would increase, resulting in higher wages for his employees. It would also fund an expansion of the company's facilities, the construction of the Rouge Complex.

Missing from the equation was the welfare of the stockholders, an omission that did not go unnoticed. In November of 1916, the Dodge brothers filed a lawsuit against Henry Ford and Ford Motor Company's other directors. At issue was the legality of Ford's system of continually reinvesting profits at the expense of paying dividends. The suit also challenged Ford's right to build the planned Rouge facilities, such as the steel mill, which were not directly related to auto assembly.

In the initial trial, the Dodge brothers prevailed, but in February 1919, the Michigan Supreme Court allowed for the construction of the Rouge facilities but ordered Ford to pay dividends on the old formula, which amounted to $19.3 million.[3]

FORD BEGINS WORK ON THE RIVER ROUGE COMPLEX

■ **AS FUNCTIONAL AS THE HIGHLAND PART PLANT WAS,** by 1916, Henry Ford was determined to build a new facility capable of even greater efficiencies. Ford believed the improvements he sought could best be achieved through vertical integration. Raw material would arrive by ship or locomotive (originating from Ford-owned mines and sawmills) to be used for manufacturing almost every needed component, emerging as a finished vehicle. Ford selected a 2,000-acre site in Dearborn along the Rouge River near its confluence with the Detroit River.

The undertaking would be huge. Work began in 1918, with significant dredging and widening of the river. Next was the sinking of thousands of pilings to support the massive buildings: blast furnaces, a steel mill, a foundry, and plants dedicated to making axles, springs, tires, and body panels, which would culminate in final assembly. Ford was so intent on achieving self-sufficiency that the facility generated its own power and even had its own police and fire departments. Construction would not be fully complete until 1927.

Simultaneous with the beginning of construction, Ford Motor Company received a contract from the Navy Department to build 112 Eagle Boats for pursuing enemy submarines. Assembly began even before the first building was complete, but World War I ended in Europe before the first boats could be delivered. Still, this feat of engineering would burnish Henry Ford's national reputation.[4]

Curiously, it would not be until 1927 that a completed car would emerge from the Rouge. For the first several years, the Model T's major components were produced at the Rouge and shipped to Highland Park for final assembly. The 1927 iteration of the Model A would be the first car totally built in Dearborn.

CONVEYORS AT THE FORD ROUGE COMPLEX
LIBRARY OF CONGRESS

43

THE DODGE BROTHERS' UNTIMELY DEATHS

■ *IN 1919, FORD DECIDED* to buy back the stock owned by outside stockholders, many of whom were among the original 1903 investors. The move cost Ford some $106 million, of which John and Horace Dodge received $25 million. Already wealthy, the transaction allowed the brothers and their families to live like European royalty.

But sadly, neither would survive to enjoy the largesse. In January of 1920, the brothers traveled to New York to participate in an automotive trade show. After attending a banquet, Horace became violently ill by the next morning. He recovered after several days, but John soon fell ill as well. Both men appeared to be stricken by either the Spanish Flu or pneumonia. John's condition continued to worsen, resulting in his death on January 14 at the age of 56.

The loss of his brother and partner was devastating to Horace. According to the January 15, 1920, edition of the *Detroit Free Press*, ". . . the two brothers were inseparable in work and play, so it is impossible to relate the history of one without mention of the other."[5] Although Horace attempted to return to work, grief over John's death exacerbated his drinking habit, , resulting in liver cirrhosis. Soon after, he contracted pneumonia. Horace died on December 10, 1920, at his winter home in Palm Beach, Florida, of complications of pneumonia and cirrhosis. He was 52.

The brothers' widows, Matilda Dodge and Anna Dodge, turned over the company's management to longtime manager Frederick Haynes. Although the company continued to prosper, by 1925, sales totaled just 200,000 cars, well below that of Ford and other competitors.[6]

On May 1, 1925, the heirs sold the Dodge Brothers Motor Car Company to the New York investment firm Dillon, Read & Company for $146 million, the largest cash transaction in American history up to that time.

JOHN AND HORACE DODGE
PUBLIC DOMAIN

GENERAL MOTORS AND THE SAGA
OF WILLIAM DURANT, PART ONE

■ *ACHIEVING SUCCESS WITH BUICK* was far too little to satisfy William Durant. Like many of his peers, he saw huge potential in the future of automobiles. But in contrast to Henry Ford, who favored one car for the masses, Durant reasoned that buyers of various means would gravitate to vehicles commensurate to their station in life.

This observation inspired the ever-ambitious Durant to use his company as the cornerstone of a constellation of automotive brands. Each would represent different price levels, with models emphasizing unique features and functionalities. After recruiting a roster of investors, the businessman formed General Motors Holding Company on September 16, 1908, as a vessel for Buick and his planned future acquisitions. GM at this time existed solely as a holding company—it conducted no business of its own.

Subsequent additions followed in rapid order. In 1908, Durant purchased a struggling

Oldsmobile from Samuel and Fred Smith. A year later, Cadillac, Oakland (later known as Pontiac), and Rapid Motor Vehicle, the forerunner of GMC Truck, were added, along with an array of obscure brands now lost to history, including Cartercar, Elmore, and Ewing. Years later, GM would deploy even more brands aimed at customers of different means. Each entity brought its unique customs and traditions, which often led to disagreements between Durant and established managers. Unaccustomed to dealing with corporate bureaucracy, Durant also endured a series of skirmishes with the GM board of directors.

Durant incurred a debt of more than $1 million on his buying spree, wreaking havoc on the company's balance sheet. In late 1910, the board forced out the creative yet foolhardy entrepreneur from Flint.

WILLIAM C. DURANT
LIBRARY OF CONGRESS

LOUIS CHEVROLET

■ *A FORMER BIKE MECHANIC* who emigrated from France by way of Canada, Louis Chevrolet liked living in the fast lane. While living in Brooklyn, New York, after the turn of the century, he drove a Fiat race car for a living. In 1905, Chevrolet defeated Barney Oldfield in a race at New York's Morris Park, reaching an astounding 68 miles per hour. He subsequently beat Walter Christie and Henry Ford in a one-mile race at Cape May, New Jersey.[7]

The quick accolades that followed attracted the eye of William Durant. In 1907, Durant, then running Buick, recruited Chevrolet for the Buick racing team. While amassing an impressive record of wins, his success came at the expense of his health, as he required an extended period to recover from racing-related injuries.

In 1909, Chevrolet set up an engine shop in Detroit. A year later, Durant again approached him with a proposal to partner, rename his business Chevrolet Motor Car Company, and develop a touring car. Legend states that wallpaper in a Paris hotel where Chevrolet once stayed inspired his company's now-famous bowtie logo.

The new vehicle, called the Series C Classic Six, debuted in 1913 to great acclaim. Its design had several innovative features, including the first floor-mounted gearshift and a counterbalanced crankshaft.[8] The car was powered with a 299-cubic-inch, six-cylinder engine built in a T-Head configuration. The new car was a success, with sales of 3,000 units its first year, despite the high price of $2,150.

In 1914, Durant wanted to add a more economical model, which Chevrolet vigorously opposed. This disagreement prompted Chevrolet to sell his interest to Durant and begin a new company, the Frontenac Motor Car Company, dedicated to crafting precision race cars.[9]

LOUIS CHEVROLET IN SUNBEAM RACE CAR

LIBRARY OF CONGRESS

GENERAL MOTORS AND THE SAGA OF WILLIAM DURANT, PART TWO

■ **DESPITE ENDURING PERSONAL MISFORTUNES,** William C. Durant lost none of his ambition after his unceremonious exit from GM. After parting with Louis Chevrolet, Durant continued the operation and successfully brought an economical car to market in 1915: the Chevrolet Series 490, a four-door touring sedan.

Intended to compete with the Ford Model T, the 490 offered an overhead valve (a design Durant strongly favored), a 2.8-liter engine that produced 24 horsepower. The car's name was also its initial price—$490. Sales were brisk. In 1916, production totaled more than 70,000 units. Profits from the vehicle caused Chevrolet's stock price to soar, enabling Durant to buy up shares in GM.

At the same time, Durant was working on assembling another company of previously independent supplier brands. His efforts led to United Motors Corporation, which included New Departure Manufacturing Company (a ball bearing manufacturer) plus two producers of starters and electric components, Remy Electric and Dayton Engineering Laboratories, the latter of which became known as Delco.

Rounding out the new venture was Hyatt Roller Bearing Company, whose president, Alfred P. Sloan, would become head of United Motors and ultimately the longtime CEO of GM.[10] The new company produced components for various automakers.

In 1918, GM purchased United Motors to establish greater vertical integration and purchased Chevrolet for its value. According to historian Arthur Pound, Chevrolet "had worked out a broadly based system of production and nationwide assembly upon which it could build its quality leadership of the future."[11] Both companies were soon folded into GM. At this time, the company's more familiar structure emerged, consisting of a centralized senior management overseeing its member companies, all of which then became divisions or subsidiaries of GM. This development returned William Durant to the chairmanship.

During his years in exile, Durant had failed to develop the virtue of discipline. Immediately after his return, he commissioned construction on the new General Motors Building on West Grand Boulevard (which he intended to name the Durant Building) while continuing on the path of acquiring additional outside companies without a coherent plan to manage them effectively.[12] A severe recession in 1920 impacted sales, but management failed to adjust production accordingly. Finally, in November of 1920, William C. Durant resigned from his role at GM—this time for good.

GM BUILDING, DETROIT
LIBRARY OF CONGRESS

WALTER CHRYSLER ORGANIZES CHRYSLER CORPORATION (MAXWELL, CHALMERS, ETC.)

■ *A MAN OF ASTOUNDING TALENTS,* Walter Chrysler can best be known as the "fixer" of the Detroit auto industry as it entered its third decade. In addition, Chrysler's level of confidence complemented his technical expertise, which made him so sought after.

Chrysler, a native of Wamego, Kansas, spent his early career in the railroad industry. While working as a manager for the American Locomotive Company, he was recruited to head production for Buick, then located in Flint. His sound management resulted in cutting costs without compromising product quality. But in 1916, when William Durant made his return to GM, Chrysler predicted a clash of cultures and tendered his resignation. Durant immediately tried to change his mind, offering Chrysler full autonomy and an astronomical salary of $120,000 per year, which he accepted.

In 1919, Chrysler left when his contract expired. Soon after, he was recruited to reorganize the Willys-Overland Company in Toledo, Ohio. He soon hired a team of three exceptional engineers from Studebaker: Fred Zeder, Owen Skelton, and Carl Breer—collectively known as the Three Musketeers. In 1920, the trio designed a car with a new six-cylinder engine, which was named "Chrysler."

Unable to secure an interest in Willys, Chrysler returned to Detroit to invest in the Maxwell Motors Company. At the time, Maxwell was embroiled in a bitter dispute with the Chalmers Motor Company, the result of an alliance that had gone sour.

Chrysler consolidated the assets of Chalmers and Maxwell while phasing out both brand names. He replaced them with Plymouth, DeSoto, and Chrysler, the higher end nameplate, christening the entire business Chrysler Corporation. In 1928, Chrysler purchased Dodge from Dillon, Read & Company (the entity that had acquired it from the Dodge widows), and it integrated into his empire.

WALTER CHRYSLER OUTSIDE THE WHITE HOUSE
LIBRARY OF CONGRESS

HENRY LELAND AND LINCOLN

■ **HENRY LELAND** left Cadillac in 1917, yet his energy and ambition remained intact. Within months, Leland and his son Wilfred founded the Lincoln Motor Company as a manufacturer of high-quality engines. Operating out of the former Warren Motor Car factory at Holden and Lincoln Streets (a lucky coincidence), the company began by building the V-12 Liberty engines the government sought from Cadillac. Less than a year later, the company moved to a newly constructed plant at West Warren and Livernois Avenues.

After the war, Leland decided to capitalize on his exceptional engineering skills and enter the luxury car market. Lincoln's first model, the "L" series, boasted a newly designed V-8 engine and an all-new suspension to produce a powerful yet smooth ride. Unfortunately, the national recession of 1920–21, corporate mismanagement, and a tax dispute with the federal government forced the young company into insolvency.

After a period of delicate negotiations, Henry Ford stepped in at the behest of his wife Clara and son Edsel to purchase Lincoln as a high-end division of Ford Motor Company. After buying the company for $8 million, Ford initially kept the Lelands on.[13] Personality conflicts quickly developed, however, resulting in the founders' dismissal after only four months, while creating a lifelong rift between the two families.

But Lincoln found an able manager in young Edsel Ford, whose interest in styling and quality made for a perfect match. Aided by Ford Motor Company's resources, the Lincoln brand flourished and remains Ford's luxury pillar today.

LINCOLN IN FRONT OF THE US CAPITOL
LIBRARY OF CONGRESS

LINCOLN ROADSTER

LIBRARY OF CONGRESS

51

GENERAL MOTORS ORGANIZES THE ART AND COLOR SECTION

■ *AS THE 1920S PROGRESSED,* the comfort of a car's driver and passenger emerged as a priority. Most earlier vehicles were designed with open-air seating, making for an unpleasant ride during inclement weather. In 1926, enclosed interiors began to appear, improving the driving experience considerably.

But this created another problem. Making the cab high enough to provide sufficient head room often resulted in vehicles up to 75 inches high, while the width of the chassis remained relatively narrow, usually no more than 70 inches. A car with a center of gravity this high posed a significant safety risk, besides being unattractive. At GM, this resulted from a lack of coordination between the engineering staff and the designers of the cars' bodies, which were supplied separately by the Fisher Body Division.

In 1926, GM Chairman Alfred Sloan took note of this issue in meetings with his senior staff. Shortly after, Lawrence Fisher, general manager of the Cadillac division, visited a dealership in California that also customized vehicles for famous Hollywood figures.[14] While there,

THE NEW EXTRA VALUE *La Salle*

Distinctive BEAUTY AND STYLE

1935 LASALLE TOURING SEDAN AD

he met a young designer named Harley Earl. Earl fashioned his designs by using techniques mostly unknown, including constructing full-size clay models, allowing him to "design the complete automobile, shaping the body, hood, fenders, headlights, and running boards into a good looking whole."[15]

Fisher recruited Earl to come to Detroit on a contract basis to work on a new model—the La Salle—to occupy a niche between Cadillac and Oldsmobile in the GM hierarchy of brands. The La Salle sported a longer and lower look than

its counterparts, deeper fenders and running boards, and a smoother overall appearance. The car was an instant success after its 1927 debut, which motivated Sloan to create a new department dedicated to automotive design. In late 1927, the Art and Color Section was created with Earl as its director. With strong support from senior management, the new unit gradually became integrated into the GM family, collaborating with the engineering and sales staffs in a coordinated fashion.

END OF THE MODEL T

■ *BY 1926,* the venerable Ford Model T had sold some 16.5 million units over its 17-year life. But by 1926, the Model T had become outdated. Competition from Chevrolet relegated Ford's car to the number two spot in sales. Reluctantly, Henry Ford began to consider a replacement car.

The result would take Ford Motor Company back to its roots, at least figuratively. After debuting the original Model A in 1903, successive Fords were branded by ascending letters of the alphabet. Following the Model A were the B, AC, C, F, K, N, R, S, and T. To emphasize the completely new design, the company opted to start the sequence over again, returning to the letter A.

15 MILLIONTH MODEL T

WALTER P. REUTHER LIBRARY, ARCHIVES OF URBAN AND LABOR AFFAIRS, WAYNE STATE UNIVERSITY

DEBUT OF THE NEW MODEL A

■ *THE 1927 FORD MODEL A* represented a turning point in the evolution of Ford vehicles. While Henry Ford had little interest in what a car looked like, his son Edsel was much more interested in automotive design. And while the Model A sported several engineering and safety improvements, the car's introduction allowed Edsel Ford to put his own creative stamp on a new vehicle, an opportunity he relished.

With an additional 24 inches in length, Model A cut a different silhouette than its predecessor. The radiator shell had a more graceful shape, with sides that angled outward and a double-curved top reminiscent of the top of a heart.[16] Edsel also oversaw the development of new color and trim options. The Model A was offered in several editions, including a coupe, convertible sedan, town car, and taxi. It was also the first car to offer safety glass for the windshield.

FORD MODEL A—MODERN IMAGE
VOLO AUTO MUSEUM

FORD MODEL A STATION WAGON
HIP POSTCARD

FORD MODEL A—MODERN IMAGE
VOLO MUSEUM

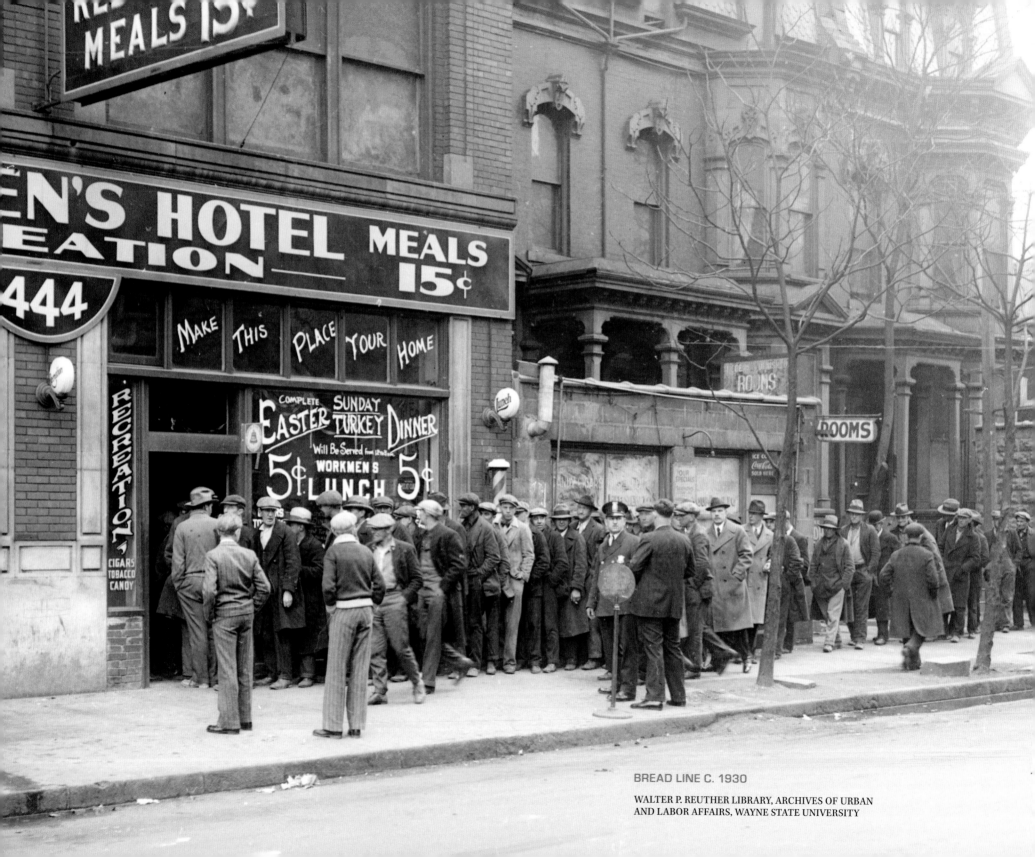

BREAD LINE C. 1930

CHAPTER FIVE

YEARS OF CONSOLIDATION AND DEPRESSION

BY 1929, the Detroit auto industry, while still supporting several small carmakers, had largely coalesced around what came to be known as the "Big Three"—General Motors (GM), Ford, and Chrysler. Meanwhile, their collective success had lifted Detroit to a level of affluence few had imagined 20 years earlier. The construction of the General Motors and Fisher Buildings, the openings of the Ambassador Bridge and Detroit-Windsor Tunnel, and the building of the Detroit Cultural Center all brought a world-class urbanity to what had been a simple workingman's town. Auto production reached some 5.3 million units, fueling record profits for the city's automakers. High-paying jobs were plentiful, with unemployment scarcely above 3%.[1]

But the seismic shift of October 1929 changed Detroit and the world forever. That month's stock market crash, which is the event generally viewed as responsible for the Great Depression, laid waste to the worldwide economy. Auto sales immediately fell, causing the Detroit automakers to lay off thousands of workers. By 1931, auto production fell to just 1.3 million vehicles.[2] By mid-1930, unemployment nationally had risen to over 15% and reached an astonishing 34% in Detroit. Unemployment and the ongoing reality of Prohibition caused violent crime to soar.

The impact on the auto industry was enormous. Many smaller automakers unable to compete were forced to liquidate, including Cord, Franklin, Peerless, Pierce-Arrow, and Stutz. But through a combination of luck and skill, each of the Big Three managed to survive. Ironically, some of the industry's most significant advances in performance, safety, and styling occurred during this era. Hydraulic brakes, radios, and interior heaters first made their appearance, while new, more aerodynamic silhouettes debuted in showrooms. GM can also be credited (or blamed) for initiating the custom of annual model years, which gave customers a reason to annually trade up to something new. What some saw as savvy marketing others viewed as planned obsolescence.

FORD AND THE 1932 HUNGER MARCH

CLIPPING FOR *DETROIT FREE PRESS*, MARCH 8, 1932

NEWSPAPERS.COM

■ *EARLY IN THE DEPRESSION,* Ford Motor Company tried to protect its employees from the economic pain. Unlike its competitors, Ford laid off few workers during 1930 while trying to maintain decent wages.[3] But as the Depression wore on into 1931 and 1932, plummeting sales forced the automaker to reduce staffing.

Meanwhile, hundreds of Detroit families had become increasingly desperate, which contributed to political instability. Magnifying the pain was the lack of unemployment insurance, Social Security, and federal guarantees on bank deposits. New Deal programs addressing these needs would not appear until years later. Political extremism soon filled this void, leading to the formation of Unemployed Councils of the USA, an outreach of the Communist Party USA.

On March 7, 1932, members of the Detroit Unemployed Council (only some of whom identified as Communists) staged a protest, marching from downtown Detroit toward the Rouge Complex along Fort Street, arriving at the Detroit-Dearborn boundary at Miller Road. Their stated goal was to personally present Henry Ford with an 11-point list of demands, which included a recall of all laid-off Ford

workers, abolition of the Service Department (a euphemistically named squad of company spies and thugs that brutally suppressed any hint of union activity), and a seven-hour workday.

Their reception was anything but cordial. Waiting at the intersection was a line of 50 Dearborn police, backed up by Ford Service Department personnel. Police deployed tear gas, most of which was dispersed by the wind. Marchers responded by throwing dirt and rocks while continuing to the plant's Gate # 3. Police and security then retreated to an overpass, from which they unleashed water cannons and submachine guns, killing five marchers and wounding 19.

Reaction in the media was mixed, with Detroit newspapers generally defending Ford's response, while national publications tended to side with the marchers. In the end, however, the incident damaged Henry Ford's reputation as a kind-hearted industrialist. The resulting ill will would spawn problems for Ford Motor Company over the coming years.

FORD V-8 CABRIOLET

■ **BY 1929,** competition between the Detroit automakers was heating up, propelling Chevrolet to develop the straight-six engine, which featured six cylinders arranged in a line driving a common crankshaft. The invention was so successful that it remained a GM mainstay until the 1950s. Ford took note and was determined to respond by introducing a V8 engine.

Work on the new engine was done in strict secrecy. Instead of working at the Ford Engineering Laboratory, Carl Schultz and Ray Laird were sequestered at Greenfield Village in Thomas Edison's laboratory, which was moved to Dearborn from Fort Myers, Florida. But despite the strict security, by late 1931, word leaked about the project, causing sales of the existing Model A to plummet.[4]

Although the pair had not yet perfected the engine, the company decided to pair it to a vehicle and market it. In January 1932, Ford unveiled the Model 18, the first mass-produced car to offer a V8 engine. The new 3.6-liter machine produced 65 horsepower, but subsequent improvements to the carburetor and ignition would augment that figure.

FORD V8 CABRIOLET ADVERTISMENT
DOCKERILLS.COM

GENERAL MOTORS AND THE 1937 SIT-DOWN STRIKE

■ *ECONOMIC HARDSHIPS FOR DETROIT* and the nation persisted and grew even more severe during the early 1930s. But despite high unemployment, limited auto production did continue. To increase productivity, managers engaged in "line speed ups" to force assembly line workers to produce more vehicles in a finite amount of time, often forcing employees to their breaking point.

The nascent unions' efforts to improve the lot of workers by striking were partially successful at some smaller companies. But in January of 1933, employees at Briggs Manufacturing, a supplier of auto bodies to Ford, struck the company's four plants. Owner Walter Briggs labeled the workers communists and used police and sheriff's deputies to disperse the strikers and escort in replacement workers. The company housed replacement workers in the plant, reducing the effectiveness of picketers.

In 1935, Congress passed the National Labor Relations Act, also known as the Wagner Act, which legalized workers' right to organize and engage in collective bargaining. That same year, the United Auto Workers (UAW) formally organized. It quickly realized that taking on large, multi-plant employers such as the Big Three would be a better strategy than striking individual shops. The union decided to focus its attention on GM, the largest employer in the industry. Union strategists, including Roy Reuther (brother of Walter Reuther), Henry Kraus, and

Wyndham Mortimer, discovered that the dies needed to stamp body parts for all Buick, Pontiac, and Oldsmobile cars originated from a plant in Flint, Fisher #1. The factory would make the ideal strike target.

The union planned to strike early in 1937, shortly after Frank Murphy, a Democrat sympathetic to the labor movement, was sworn in as governor of Michigan. On December 30, however, union leaders discovered the company's plan to move the dies early the next day. Off-shift plant employees immediately forced their way into the facility and occupied it, which was a novel idea thought to be more effective than staging a picket line. By barricading themselves in the plant, they could keep replacement workers from entering.

The strikers maintained their stance for 44 days, living off complementary meals sent in by a local restaurant. Police made a few attempts to remove the workers, but to no avail. Governor Murphy even sent in the Michigan National Guard to protect the occupants. Meanwhile, the strike spread to other GM facilities in Flint.

After tense negotiations, the company capitulated on February 11, agreeing to recognize the UAW as the legitimate representative of the hourly workers. Workers were also granted a 5% raise, while open discussion of unionism was no longer penalized.

WORKERS READING NEWSPAPER
DURING FLINT SIT-DOWN STRIKE
LIBRARY OF CONGRESS

THE BATTLE OF THE OVERPASS AT THE ROUGE

■ **FOR THE UAW,** achieving recognition at GM was a tremendous accomplishment. In the aftermath, Walter Reuther and other union officials set their sights on Ford, but they knew full well that Dearborn's family-owned company would be a much more formidable challenge. Henry Ford had been bitterly resistant to labor unions for several reasons. In addition to the expected opposition to outsiders interfering with his business, Ford harbored suspicions of a more sinister nature.

In Henry Ford's mind, labor unions had formed secret alliances with banks, Wall Street, the federal government, and the Du Pont family,[5] which was heavily invested in GM and operated its own company supplying munitions to the military. "Financiers are behind the unions and their object is to kill competition so as to reduce the income of the workers and eventually bring on war," Ford was quoted as saying.[6] At the same time, however, another faction within the company expressed a willingness to at least hold discussions with the union, including Ford's son Edsel and his wife, Clara.

Ford enforced his opposition through a network of company spies and thugs who were quick to fire or brutalize anyone even suspected of pro-union activity. Supervising this group, euphemistically titled the "Service Department," was Harry Bennett, a former boxer hired by Ford in 1921. Social attitudes regarding organized labor had changed

REUTHER AND FRANKENSTEEN AFTER BEING BEATEN

WALTER P. REUTHER LIBRARY, ARCHIVES OF URBAN AND LABOR AFFAIRS, WAYNE STATE UNIVERSITY

considerably since the beginning of the Depression, but this meant little to Bennett, who had his men impose harsh discipline with quick dispatch.

As a result, most Ford workers were largely unaware of the UAW. To address this, Walter Reuther and his deputy Richard Frankensteen planned a leafleting campaign at the Ford Rouge plant for May 26, 1937. Dozens of UAW volunteers came out to distribute literature to interested employees at shift change. The union representatives were careful to remain on public property, including the pedestrian overpass over Miller Road, a spot recommended by *Detroit News* photographer James R. Kilpatrick. While Kilpatrick was shooting images of Reuther, Frankensteen, and others, a squad of Service Department men appeared and savagely beat the union officials. They then proceeded to attack members of the media, exposing film and confiscating notebooks.

Kilpatrick, however, managed to slip away unnoticed amid the mayhem. Upon reaching his car, he directed his driver to leave immediately. Moments later, the two were stopped by a Ford security guard who demanded their photographic plates. Kilpatrick complied, and the car was allowed to proceed. It turned out, however, that the

plates the photographer surrendered were blanks. He had hidden the exposed ones under the seat. Once developed, the images showing the Ford Service personnel's cruelty were soon seen worldwide and seriously damaged Ford Motor Company's reputation.

In 1937, there was no Pulitzer Prize for photography, but Kilpatrick's work inspired its establishment. It was first awarded in 1942 to Milton Brooks, also of the *Detroit News*, for his landmark image 'Ford Strikers Riot,' which depicts striking Ford employees attacking a replacement worker—a stunning display of irony.

BUICK SERIES 40

■ **DESPITE THE ECONOMIC CALAMITY** confronting the nation, Detroit's automakers tried to maintain sales. In July 1929, Buick introduced its 1930 lineup, the Series 40, 50, and 60. Of these, the Series 40, which replaced the earlier Series 116, proved the most successful— by Depression standards. Buick offered the Series 40 in two open models: a two-passenger roadster and a four-passenger Phaeton, priced at $1,310, slightly higher than the Marquette, Buick's entry-level vehicle.

The car had a lower profile than its predecessor, with a 118-inch wheelbase on wooden spoke artillery wheels. It was equipped with an overhead-valve six-cylinder engine capable of delivering 80.5 horsepower to hold down the price. Thanks to improved styling, the Phaeton edition sported an up-to-date look, which could be enhanced with available options, including wire spoke wheels, wind wings, and exterior chrome horns.

Introducing the more affordable Series 40 when it did proved fortuitous, as it outpaced its larger cousins in sales. Buick moved 3,639 copies of the roadster, which, surprisingly, was a strong showing for a new model in 1930.[7]

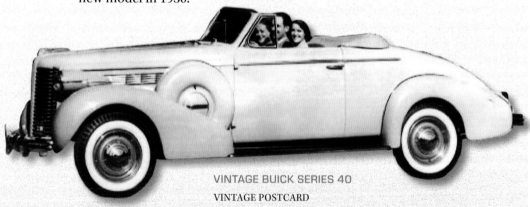

VINTAGE BUICK SERIES 40
VINTAGE POSTCARD

THE CHRYSLER AIRFLOW

■ **AS THE DEPRESSION CONTINUED** into 1934, Chrysler decided the time was right to introduce its latest brainchild: a design to harness the natural movement of air surrounding a car. The idea was to produce a design that would yield greater efficiency while offering the customer something new in the way of styling and interior features. The central idea behind the car became its name, the Chrysler Airflow.

After several years of research, Chrysler engineers learned of the considerable air resistance created by the motion of a car traveling above 25 miles per hour. This was due to the high, imposing grills and tall body styles characteristic of traditional cars. In fact, they discovered the cars were more aerodynamic if driven backwards.

In addition, passenger compartments were typically located over the axles. When passengers occupied the back seats, 75% of the total weight was situated over the rear wheels, presenting a high risk of the vehicle flipping over.

The findings led the automaker to produce a revolutionary new design. The central feature was its "waterfall" grill that curved upward to form the hood, allowing the car to better harness the air. In addition, the engine was placed over the front axle while the rear seat was moved forward, within the car's wheelbase. The modifications resulted in superior aerodynamics, more agile handling, and improved safety. An all-steel frame (another first) of unibody construction was also introduced. At the time, more traditional cars still used wood for some structural components.

The interior styling features mimicked the newly popular art deco movement of the time. For its debut year of 1934, the Airflow was offered in two-door coupe and four-door sedan versions, each powered by a flathead eight-cylinder engine.

Unfortunately, the public was put off by the unconventional new car. First year sales were less than 11,000 units. Over the next few years, Chrysler modified the styling more in line with consumer tastes, including a peaked grill. Despite these efforts, the car never became a sales success. After the 1937 model year, the Airflow was retired.

But despite its failure, the Chrysler Airflow's engineering innovations proved groundbreaking and eventually became commonplace in competitors' models. Later designs offered by Volvo, Volkswagen, and others reflect the Airflow's influence.

1937 AIRFLOW COUPE ON DISPLAY AT THE CHRYSLER BUILDING IN NEW YORK CITY

LIBRARY OF CONGRESS

THE EVOLUTION OF STYLE AT FORD:
A 1929 MODEL A NEXT TO A 1939
STANDARD

WALTER P. REUTHER LIBRARY, ARCHIVES
OF URBAN AND LABOR AFFAIRS, WAYNE
STATE UNIVERSITY

GENERAL MOTORS CARAVAN OF PROGRESS

■ **FEW THINGS FASCINATE AMERICANS** more than a contemplation of "the future," technological or otherwise. This magnetism was enshrined at the 1933 Chicago World's Fair, formally known as A Century of Progress International Exhibition, celebrated to commemorate the city's centennial. Detroit's auto industry was well represented. Lincoln displayed one of its first concept cars, Nash presented its latest lineup, and Cadillac introduced the new V-16 limousine, in addition to exhibits showcasing emerging technologies such as high-compression car engines and diesel–electric hybrid locomotives.[8] The event was a tremendous success, owing perhaps to the distraction it offered amid the Depression.

Charles Kettering, vice president of research at GM, was sad to see the event end. He proposed taking the exhibits on a roadshow, visiting smaller cities and towns to allow locals to see GM innovation firsthand. The result was the General Motors Caravan of Progress. Eight

GENERAL MOTORS CARAVAN OF PROGRESS (CONTINUED)

customized "Streamliners" were built by the company's Yellow Coach Division to transport the exhibits. Deluxe versions of five cars, one each from Chevrolet, Pontiac, Oldsmobile, Buick, and Cadillac/LaSalle, were selected.

The campaign was hugely successful. From 1936 to 1940, the Caravan visited 251 communities in the United States, Mexico, and Cuba and was seen by more than 12.5 million people. [9] An updated version of the event, the

Parade of Progress, began in 1940 but was soon terminated due to World War II. In the 1950s, the Parade saw a revival, and for a short time, it coincided with the GM Motorama.

GM FUTURELINER
LIBRARY OF CONGRESS

RECOGNITION OF THE UAW AT FORD IN 1941

■ **THE VIOLENCE OF MAY 1937** increased the acrimony between Henry and Edsel Ford. And while the anti-union forces had won the day, the tide continued to shift. In 1939, the company was found to have violated the Wagner Act in federal district court. The circuit court of appeals reaffirmed the ruling, while the US Supreme Court declined to review the case.[10]

Tensions between a recalcitrant Ford Motor Company and an equally determined UAW continued to escalate through 1939 and 1940. By April of 1941, workers at the Rouge had grown weary of the company's heavy-handed tactics. Although fewer than a third were union members, on April 1, the UAW called for a strike. Most workers honored the walkout, except for a large percentage of African American employees. Over the years, Ford had been willing to hire black workers when other companies would not, instilling loyalty to Henry Ford. Some did try to cross the picket line, only to face violent reprisals.

Despite the lack of complete support, the strike dragged on into late May. Henry Ford was willing to close the plant permanently, so intense was his opposition to the union. But the rift within the Ford family, pitting Henry and Harry Bennett against Edsel and Clara, finally boiled over. In an act of incredible bravery, Clara played her ultimate trump card. Unless her husband negotiated a settlement with the union, she would petition for divorce. Only then did Henry Ford relent.[11]

On May 26, a vote was held, which resulted in an overwhelming victory for the UAW. The parties signed a contract on June 20. Paradoxically, Henry Ford agreed to terms more generous than those sought by the union. Ford workers were to be paid more than their GM and Chrysler counterparts, and workers unfairly terminated for union sympathies were rehired.[12]

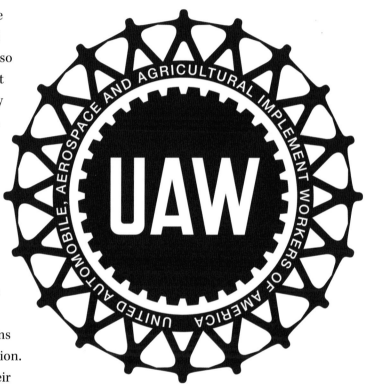

SEAL OF U.S. WAR PRODUCTION BOARD

CHAPTER SIX

WORLD WAR II AND THE ARSENAL OF DEMOCRACY

SHORTLY AFTER the auto unions achieved recognition by the Big Three and secured the right to collective bargaining, the onset of hostilities due to World War II would reshape Detroit's signature industry.

The calamity forced automakers to embark on the most extraordinary industrial transition in American history. From early 1940 until mid-1945, the auto industry would produce *no* cars for civilian use. Political turmoil in Europe and the Far East would morph into extreme militarism, forcing democratic nations to rescue the free world.

Early on, federal military planners recognized the unique ability of the nation's auto manufacturers to supply the nation's armed forces with the hardware and munitions needed to effectively defend against the enemy. The fact that much of the industry was centered in southeast Michigan made for more efficient logistics and easier lines of communication.

ROLE OF WILLIAM KNUDSEN

■ *IN THE EARLY MONTHS* of 1940, the situation in Europe turned especially grim. In the spring, Germany invaded Norway and Denmark, followed in May by its *blitzkrieg*, or lightning war, in which it overtook France and the Low Countries in a mere seven weeks. Washington immediately sensed the growing threat to the United States, prompting President Franklin Roosevelt to embark on a crash program of rearmament. At the time, the US military had a mere 500 warplanes. Roosevelt felt it needed 50,000. When he asked his longtime advisor Bernard Baruch to recommend three top candidates to coordinate the program, he responded by saying, "First, Knudsen; second, Knudsen; third, Knudsen."[1]

William Knudsen, who had risen through the ranks at Ford, left for GM in 1922 after a falling out with Henry Ford. At GM, he worked in the Chevrolet division before being appointed company president in 1937. Aside from his success in the auto industry, he was deeply affected by the Nazi invasion of his native Denmark.

Knudsen answered the president's call and left for Washington to take his position as chairman of the Office of Production Management and serve as a member of the National Defense Advisory Commission. En route, he stopped in New York to share his decision with Chairman Alfred Sloan, who was bitterly opposed to Knudsen's departure.

WILLIAM KNUDSEN
LIBRARY OF CONGRESS

Knudsen significantly improved the military's procurement of war material from the private sector. His automotive connections gave him considerable influence, enabling him to ramp up the production of ships, tanks, and planes with astonishing speed. After the war, when asked what was most instrumental in the Allied victory, Knudsen replied, "We won because we smothered the enemy in an avalanche of production, the like of which he had never seen, nor dreamed possible."[2]

ROLLS-ROYCE ENGINES BY PACKARD

■ *AS 1940 DRAGGED ON,* Great Britain's need for US military hardware under the Lend-Lease Act grew ever more acute. One example was their desperate need for modified Rolls-Royce Merlin engines for their planes, including the Supermarine Spitfire fighter and Avro Lancaster bomber. But during Knudsen's early months in Washington, a coordinated system for procurement did not yet exist. To bypass this obstacle, he directly approached Ford and negotiated a contract with Charles Sorensen and Edsel Ford for 9,000 engines.[3]

ROLLS ROYCE ENGINE QUALITY
CHECKERS AT PACKARD
LIBRARY OF CONGRESS

But no sooner had the deal been announced than Henry Ford, who remained very much in charge at Ford Motor Company, abruptly canceled the agreement, proclaiming, "We are not doing business with the British government or any other foreign government."[4] Historians debate as to Ford's motivation—it could be his professed pacifism, isolationism, or a hidden pro-Nazi bias.

Knudsen contacted Alvin Macauley, president of Packard, who agreed to take on the job out of desperation. Their execution was so flawless that orders for more continued to pour in. The innovative engine (originally designed for air racing and not for combat) delivered over 1,000 horsepower and was so well regarded that North American Aviation adopted it for their P-51 Mustang fighter used by the US Army Air Forces.

This was not the first time Packard took on defense work. During the interwar period, the company also produced aircraft engines for the US military—a fact it made known in its advertising.

ROLLS-ROYCE ENGINE
ASSEMBLY AT PACKARD

LIBRARY OF CONGRESS

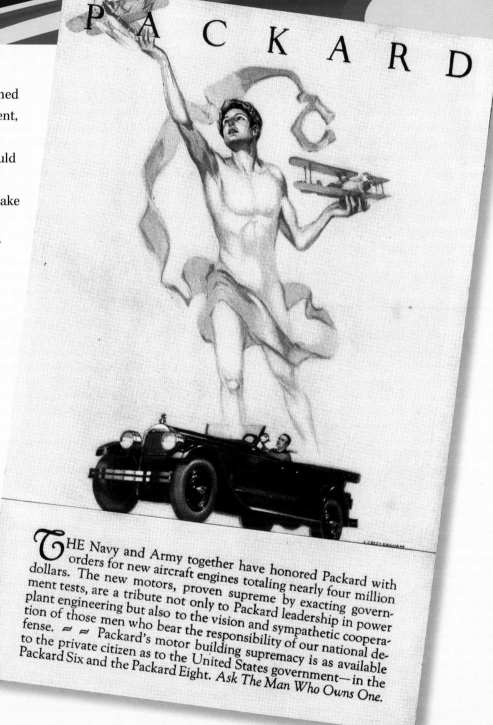

1926 PACKARD AD

HIP POSTCARD

PACKARD

THE Navy and Army together have honored Packard with orders for new aircraft engines totaling nearly four million dollars. The new motors, proven supreme by exacting government tests, are a tribute not only to Packard leadership in power plant engineering but also to the vision and sympathetic cooperation of those men who bear the responsibility of our national defense. ≈ ≈ Packard's motor building supremacy is as available to the private citizen as to the United States government—in the Packard Six and the Packard Eight. *Ask The Man Who Owns One.*

PEARL HARBOR AND ITS IMPACT

■ **FOR SEVERAL YEARS,** Japan had emerged as a growing threat to peace in eastern Asia. Following its invasions of Manchuria in 1931 and French Indochina in 1940, the United States responded with a partial trade embargo to forestall further aggression by the island nation. As tensions rose, negotiations between the two countries aimed at defusing the situation continued through 1941. As the discussions dragged on inconclusively, a secret convoy of Japanese warships sailed toward Hawaii while Japanese diplomats in Washington continued to negotiate in bad faith.

On Sunday, December 7, 1941, more than 400 Japanese fighter planes launched from six aircraft carriers carried out a surprise attack on the US Naval Fleet at Pearl Harbor, Hawaii. The assault killed some 2,400 Americans and destroyed or damaged 18 vessels. The next day, Congress declared war on Japan, thrusting the United States into World War II.

Immediately, the calamity had a galvanizing effect on the nation, creating a strong sense of unity and eliminating any remaining isolationism. While the Roosevelt administration had been preparing for what it thought was inevitable US involvement in the war, the nation now saw that all Americans' energy and ingenuity would need to achieve a common goal. And the industrial might of Detroit's auto industry was ready to help.

Although Big Three workers had only recently won union recognition, labor leaders wasted no time acknowledging the urgent national priority. Within just 48 hours of the attack, officials of the American Federation of Labor (AFL) and the Congress of Industrial Organizations (CIO), of which the UAW was a member, voluntarily took a "no strike" pledge for the duration of the war.[5]

PEARL HARBOR ATTACK
LIBRARY OF CONGRESS

ARMAMENTS PRODUCED BY GENERAL MOTORS

■ *KNUDSEN'S COMPREHENSIVE UNDERSTANDING* of the auto industry allowed him to know where to go for whatever he needed. GM, his old company, was alone given contracts to provide an astonishing array of hardware. According to the GM Heritage Center, the automaker churned out 13,000 Navy fighter planes and torpedo bombers, 301,000 aircraft gyrocompasses, 206,000 aircraft engines, 198,000 diesel engines, 854,000 trucks of various sizes, 1.9 million machine guns, 11 million fuses, and much more.

While the company produced most of this material under government-mandated low-profit contracts, the enormous volume made the venture nonetheless lucrative. From 1942 to 1945, GM's sales exceeded $13.4 billion, yielding profits of more than $673 million, a 50% increase from its prewar high.[6]

GM INSPECTOR CHECKING
MACHINE GUN BARRELS

LIBRARY OF CONGRESS

GM DEMONSTRATION OF MILITARY VEHICLES

WALTER P. REUTHER LIBRARY, ARCHIVES OF URBAN AND LABOR AFFAIRS, WAYNE STATE UNIVERSITY

FORD WILLOW RUN PLANT AND THE B-24 LIBERATOR

■ **ON THE EVE OF US INVOLVEMENT** in the war, American military strength was embarrassingly weak. An acute lack of airpower was especially problematic, given that military planners predicted air dominance would be essential to victory. Yet the Army Air Corps had only 1,200 planes at its disposal, only some of which were combat ready. An estimated 50,000 planes of various types would be needed.

In 1940, Secretary of War Henry Stimson commissioned businessman Robert Lovett to assess the capabilities of American aircraft factories. His report was bleak and indicated a severe lack of production capacity.

To meet the need, William Knudsen suggested that automotive plants be retooled to produce aircraft. He felt that only the vast resources of the industry could deliver the quantity needed. Ford was assigned the B-24 Liberator Bomber, designed by the Consolidated Aircraft Company of

San Diego, California. A January 1941 visit to the Consolidated facility by Edsel Ford and Charles Sorensen quickly shocked the visitors from Michigan. Production was slow and inefficient. Planes were built by hand, lacking uniformity.

The men returned to their hotel, and Sorensen stayed up the entire night conceiving a plan for efficiently building B-24s on a moving assembly line, ensuring the quantity the military needed. He even sketched out a mammoth plant to house the operation. Edsel Ford approved the plan, and in April 1941, construction began at Willow Run, a tranquil area near Ypsilanti that had been home to a Ford farm and a summer camp for boys. An airfield was built adjacent to the plant.

By September, the five-million-square-foot facility was complete. But achieving sufficient production levels proved challenging, as adapting a method used to build cars to assembling an aircraft with more than 450,000 parts was complicated and difficult. A steady stream of design changes, time-consuming training, and high employee turnover were just some of the obstacles. The plant was not able to deliver its first bomber until October 1942.

But Charles Sorensen persisted, even after Edsel Ford's untimely death in May of 1943. By mid-1944, the coveted goal of one bomber per hour was finally reached. By June of 1945, the plant had produced more than 8,800 planes, over 50% of the B-24s built in the United States. Despite the Ford family's drama, their namesake company's contribution to military aviation ranks as one of the private industry's most impactful wartime achievements.

COMPLETED B-24 LIBERATORS ON
TARMAC AT WILLOW RUN

LIBRARY OF CONGRESS

PRODUCTION OF B-24 LIBERATORS AT
WILLOW RUN

WALTER P. REUTHER LIBRARY, ARCHIVES
OF URBAN AND LABOR AFFAIRS, WAYNE
STATE UNIVERSITY

CHRYSLER WARREN TANK PLANT

■ **BEFORE WORLD WAR II,** military strategists did not see a need for large numbers of tanks on a battlefield. That perception quickly changed early in the conflict when reports first came in of the Nazi Blitzkrieg attacks. With armored assets, the Germans were able to conquer France and the Low Countries in a mere 46 days in the spring of 1940. The Roosevelt administration, which strongly suspected the United States would soon enter the war, included tanks in the Arsenal of Democracy.

William Knudsen, mining his network of automotive connections, called on K. T. Keller, chairman of Chrysler Corporation. Asked if his company could mass-produce tanks, Keller immediately accepted the challenge. The executive immediately sent his engineers to the Army's tank arsenal in Rock Island, Illinois, to study the M2A1 medium-duty tank design. Taking blueprints with them, the team returned to Detroit, constructed a full-size wooden model, and laid out plans for producing tanks in mass numbers.

An agreement was negotiated between the automaker and the military, under which the government would build and equip a dedicated tank plant while Chrysler would operate it. Soon, architect Albert Kahn was commissioned to design the enormous facility. Ground was broken in what was then rural Warren Township in September 1940, and work continued through the following winter, despite the hardships imposed by the bitter cold.[7] Machinery was moved in even before construction was finished.

TANK ASSEMBLY AT CHRYSLER
LIBRARY OF CONGRESS

By April 1941, the plant was complete. Over one million square feet, five city blocks long and two deep, the facility was delivered in just eight months. Built to withstand aerial attacks, the plant featured three-foot-thick concrete walls and an angled roof capable of deflecting bombs away from the structure.

Amazingly, the first tanks rolled off the production line before the building was even completed. On April 11, 1941, the first tank emerged off the line. Five hundred units had been built by the December attack on Pearl Harbor. Throughout the war, the Detroit Arsenal Tank Plant produced a succession of newer vehicles, totaling more than 22,000 by the end of the war. Unlike the Willow Run Bomber Plant, the Warren facility continued its original function after the end of the war, building many of the military's armored vehicles during the postwar era.

THE WILLYS MB AND THE FORD GPW (AKA JEEP)

■ **AS WAR BEGAN** to erupt in Europe, US military planners recognized the changing nature of modern warfare. Based on commanders' experiences in World War I, they realized the need for a small, versatile utility vehicle useful for reconnaissance, movement of small arms, and transporting officers in the field.

Inspired by the Austin 7 used by the British Army, in early 1940, commanders at Fort Benning, Georgia, approached American Bantam Company of Butler, Pennsylvania

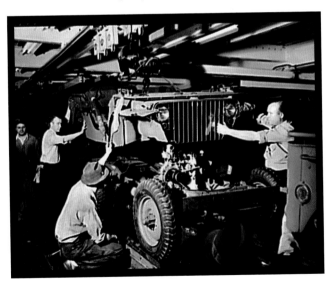

JEEP ASSEMBLY AT THE ROUGE

LIBRARY OF CONGRESS

(Austin's corporate successor), and negotiated a contract to draw up specifications for a military version of the Austin.

The government then organized a competition for a prototype. The model presented by American Bantam (AB), developed by a committee of engineers including AB's Harold Crist and freelancer Karl Probst, emerged as the winning design (Willys-Overland was the only other entrant). The concept fulfilled the Army's requirements, including four-wheel drive, a maximum wheelbase of 80 inches, and a 45-horsepower engine. Many of the components were sourced from commercially available off-the-shelf parts, which shortened the time needed for production to ramp up.

Although AB drew the winning design and produced the initial prototype, the government (which considered itself the design owner) invited AB, Willys, and Ford to each build several hundred prototypes for testing. All three complied, although each model differed slightly from the others. Eventually, all three companies produced more than 4,400 units

during preproduction, most of which were given to Great Britain and the Soviet Union under the Lend-Lease Act.

In early 1941, the Willys version was ultimately chosen for full production of the Jeep (known internally as the Willys MB), but it soon became apparent that Willys alone could not meet the military's demands. In October, Ford was contracted to build additional units, which it identified as the Ford GPW. Between the two companies, more than 647,000 copies of the vehicle were supplied to the military.

The highly versatile Jeep (as it came to be known) exceeded the military's expectations and was lauded by Army Chief of Staff General George Marshall as "America's greatest contribution to modern warfare." Jeeps could be fitted with an assortment of weapons, modified into field ambulances, or outfitted with tracks in place of wheels for operation in deep snow or mud. But perhaps the best testimony to the Jeep's durability is its postwar life as a civilian sport utility vehicle, which continues today.

TENSION BETWEEN FATHER AND SON

■ **FOR MOST OF HIS LIFE,** Edsel Ford, while dedicated to the auto business, nonetheless displayed different interests and passions than his eccentric father. While Henry approached every problem with an eye toward improved efficiency, Edsel emphasized aesthetics by developing the art of automotive styling.

Moreover, their differing perspectives affected general views on life. Henry's subordinates reflected his way of thinking. Harry Bennett, for example, was given broad latitude to rough up and even brutalize employees expressing even a hint of union sympathies. Edsel represented a more enlightened way of thinking, advocating a conciliatory approach to labor issues and an aggressive approach to improving quality.

Personality differences such as these proved to be the root of years of conflict between the two men, which ended in tragedy. While Henry had installed his son as president of Ford Motor Company in 1920, the title was merely nominal. Although Henry was without an official post, he remained very much in charge. Edsel did work to steer the company away from insolvency during the darkest years of the Depression.

Still, the stress of the experience, plus ongoing labor problems and constant browbeating from his father, negatively impacted his health. Although he had no medical expertise, Henry insisted that his son's problems were due to his errant lifestyle. He felt that if Edsel changed his eating habits and abstained from all alcohol, his health would improve.

By early 1942, Ford was producing only military hardware under strict government oversight. These responsibilities, plus the added burden of the B-24 program (which Henry refused to involve himself in), placed even more stress on Edsel. To fill the void, Charles Sorensen performed much of the company's day-to-day management.

In January, Edsel underwent surgery for severe stomach ulcers. While initially successful, his health took another blow in November when he was diagnosed with undulant fever from consuming unpasteurized milk from the Ford farm. Henry believed pasteurization was unnecessary and harmful.

By late 1942, Edsel's health had declined to the point where he considered resigning but

EDSEL FORD

stayed out of a sense of duty. Edsel would be diagnosed with stomach cancer in the coming months, the primary cause of his death on May 26, 1943.

EDSEL AND HENRY FORD
WALTER P. REUTHER LIBRARY, ARCHIVES
OF URBAN AND LABOR AFFAIRS, WAYNE
STATE UNIVERSITY

TRAFFIC ON THE JOHN C.
LODGE FREEWAY, C. 1965

CHAPTER SEVEN

THE POSTWAR YEARS

THE SUMMER OF 1945 brought global peace and ushered in a new era. The end of hostilities was followed by a permanent shift in the nation's trajectory, as emerging social and economic changes affected every corner of American life—and the auto industry was no exception. After 15 years of Depression and war, Americans were anxious to leave their hardships behind and embrace a future marked by hope and optimism. This spirit was reflected in the beefy, gas-guzzling behemoths of the 1950s, as auto ownership became a status symbol. In 1950, approximately 40 million cars were on America's roads, a figure that would double over the following decade.[1] The genre of the American sports car was born in 1953 with the debut of the Chevrolet Corvette.

The American approach stood in sharp contrast to cars built across the Atlantic. After recovering from the war, European automakers took a more thoughtful approach by building more agile, fuel-efficient vehicles.

After producing only war material for several years, Detroit's automakers were anxious to return to the business of designing, building, and selling cars—and so was the motoring public. At the end of the war, 25 million vehicles were on the road, but many were nearing the end of their useful lives.[2] By late 1945, minimal production had resumed, although most of these cars were just modified versions of prewar models.[3]

But given the extreme level of pent-up demand, virtually any vehicle was sold almost immediately after coming off the assembly line. With plenty of business to go around, the early postwar years emerged as the prosperous yet brief era of Detroit's "independent" automakers. Smaller than their big three counterparts, these second-tier manufacturers were founded earlier in the 20th century, but for various reasons never witnessed the meteoric growth seen by their peers.

Because these companies often lacked the engineering and design resources possessed by the Big Three, they generally catered to a specific market niche. But despite these limitations, independent automakers were responsible for many postwar innovations in safety, comfort, and performance, which contributed significantly to the industry's ongoing evolution.

The early postwar years also produced significant engineering and product breakthroughs at the Big Three. Cadillac introduced the overhead valve V8 engine in 1949; in 1951, Chrysler offered its V8 Firepower engine using hemispherical combustion chambers, which came to be known as the Hemi. Automatic transmissions, air conditioning, power steering, and seat belts also made their debut to enhance passenger comfort.

POSTWAR AUTOMOTIVE DESIGN

■ **WORLD WAR II'S DOMESTIC LEGACY** included a civilian workforce with burgeoning savings accounts and a population that wanted to forget the agony and hardships of war and look toward the future with hope and optimism. Meanwhile, the car was beginning to occupy a much more integral role in American life.

Sensing a longing for something new, executives at the Big Three hired scores of new designers in the years following the war. Many were veterans who attended college on the GI Bill and had studied art and design. Their energy unleashed an explosion of creativity in the design studios of Detroit's automakers. Examples included the famous tailfins introduced by Harley Earl and GM and the "Forward Look" spearheaded by Virgil Exner at Chrysler. Exner redrew rooflines to give a sleeker, more aerodynamic look.

The period also introduced scores of outlandish concept designs, producing vehicles that looked indistinguishable from spaceships. Automotive historian Greg Salustro summed up the spirit of the times in an interview to promote his film *American Dreaming*, a tribute to the hundreds of talented designers that toiled during that era:

There was an explosion of money after WWII, and America was an economic superpower. People wanted things that were modern and futuristic. It was a time when we looked forward and embraced the future, because we had a sense that the future was going to be better. That might be why a million people still gather on Woodward Avenue and stand in the hot sun all day to watch cars go by. There is a sense that there was something there, a response to that design—why we fell in love with those cars.[4]

PONTIAC HEADLIGHT AD, 1960

HIP POSTCARD

1951 GM CONCEPT CAR

GETTY IMAGES

PRESTON TUCKER

■ **BEFORE AND DURING WORLD WAR II,** Preston Tucker spent little time outside of his workshop. After spending his early career as a police officer, Tucker engaged in a series of pursuits, each capitalizing on his innate talents: car salesman, inventor, and entrepreneur. Among his concepts were engines for race cars, armored combat vehicles for military use that moved on wheels instead of tracks, a motorized gun turret for combat aircraft, and even a lightweight fighter plane, the Tucker XP-57. But despite being an engineering visionary, he was rarely able to successfully market his inventions, mostly due to failed business partnerships.

Despite this unimpressive track record, light bulbs went off in his mind as the war neared its end. Tucker saw the vast market for new automobiles and thought the time was right for an entirely new type of car with cutting-edge styling and engineering, plus the latest in safety technology. He felt that Detroit's legacy automakers, because of their dominance in the market, had become arrogant—consumed only with profit while caring little about passenger safety.

Tucker decided to produce and market a car of his own design and soon formed the Tucker Corporation.

Tucker partnered with designer George Lawson in 1944, and the duo created a concept called the Tucker Torpedo. Featuring massive front and rear fenders, an aerodynamic body shape, and a wraparound windshield, the design lived only on paper, as a prototype was never built. After Lawson left the company in late 1946, Tucker replaced him with Alex Tremulis, who was contracted for three months and refined Lawson's work. Tremulis's work featured prominently in early advertisements, but at the same time, Tucker hired yet another team of designers. A short time later, Tremulis returned, and the final design was a combination of the two teams' work.

The finished product, called the Tucker 48, included a rear-mounted six-cylinder, 335-cubic-inch engine that produced 168 horsepower. Padded dashboard and doors, seat belts, a windshield that would pop out in a collision, and a "crash chamber"—an open space on the front seat floor where passengers could duck for protection—were among the safety features offered. Perhaps the most innovative idea was a third headlight, positioned in the center of the car's front end that would pivot during turns.

Effective early publicity generated massive interest from prospective dealers. Tucker used this notoriety to begin raising capital by selling dealership franchises. The company then leased a former Dodge factory in Chicago from the US government and began to plan for production.

But Tucker soon realized he needed still more cash. To meet this need, he began an innovative "accessories program" that offered future owners the option to buy Tucker branded merchandise (floor mats, luggage, etc.) before taking delivery of the car.

The Security and Exchange Commission soon became suspicious and began investigating the Tucker Corporation. The SEC deemed the accessories program fraudulent, which greatly upset Tucker. At the same time, questionable actions by politicians hampered the company's efforts to obtain needed raw materials.

Tucker felt so strongly that he aired his grievances in, "An Open Letter to the American Industry in the Interests of the American Motorist by Preston Tucker," which ran in newspapers nationwide on June 15, 1948. But it was to no avail. In 1949, federal agents seized the company's assets. Tucker and six of his executives were indicted on charges of mail fraud and conspiracy. Tucker was eventually acquitted on all counts, but it was too late, and Tucker Corporation was liquidated. Only 51 Tucker cars were ever built, most of which now reside in museums and private collections.

UNITED STATES PATENT OFFICE

154,192

DESIGN FOR AN AUTOMOBILE

Preston T. Tucker, Ypsilanti, Mich., assignor to
Tucker Corporation, Chicago, Ill., a corporation
of Delaware

Application March 15, 1947, Serial No. 137,626

Term of patent 3½ years

(Cl. D14—3)

To all whom it may concern:

Be it known that I, Preston T. Tucker, a citizen of the United States, residing at Ypsilanti, in the county of Washtenaw and State of Michigan, have invented a new, original, and ornamental Design for an Automobile, of which the following is a specification, reference being had to the accompanying drawings, forming a part thereof, wherein:

Figure 1 is a view in side elevation of an automobile embodying the design of this invention;

Figure 2 is a top plan view;

Figure 3 is a view in front elevation; and

Figure 4 is a rear end elevational view.

The characteristic features of my design reside in the portions shown by means of full lines in the drawings.

I claim:

The ornamental design for an automobile, substantially as shown and described.

PRESTON T. TUCKER.

REFERENCES CITED

The following references are of record in the file of this patent:

UNITED STATES PATENTS

Number	Name	Date
D. 139,636	Walker	Dec. 5, 1944
D. 149,824	Lawson	June 1, 1948

OTHER REFERENCES

L'Auto Carrosserie, No. 137, September-October, 1938, page 12343, Planche 845 at top of page.

Washington Daily News, Monday, January 7, 1946, illustration entitled "Autos of the Future—Maybe."

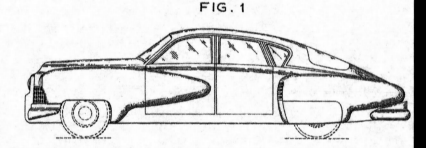

FIG. 1

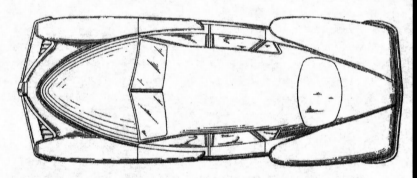

FIG. 2

INVENTOR
PRESTON T. TUCKER
BY
Toulmin & Toulmin
ATTORNEYS

FIG. 3

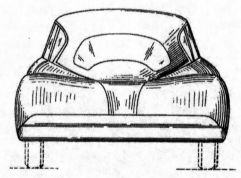

FIG. 4

FORMATION OF AMERICAN MOTORS—MERGER OF HUDSON WITH NASH-KELVINATOR

■ **THE EMERGING TREND** of postwar industry consolidation in the auto industry began in 1954 with the merger of Hudson Motors with Nash-Kelvinator of Kenosha, Wisconsin. Nash-Kelvinator itself resulted from a 1937 merger between Nash Motors and the Kelvinator Company, a manufacturer of commercial and household refrigerators.

At the time of the 1954 affiliation, both companies boasted long automotive legacies. Nash had origins dating to 1916 when former GM president Charles Nash purchased the Thomas B. Jeffery Company of Kenosha. Over the next several years, his company built the four-wheel-drive Jeffery Quad for the US military, a series of roadsters and touring cars, and an entry-level model known as the Ajax. Upon his 1937 retirement, Nash recruited Kelvinator president George W. Mason as his successor. Mason, however, would acquiesce only if the automaker merged with his company.

Hudson Motors began in Detroit in 1909 and was named for retailer Joseph Lowthian Hudson, a member of the consortium of founding investors. Roy Chapin, a protégé of Ransom Olds, was named president. The company concentrated on small, economical cars, including the six-cylinder Essex Coach. Hudson's introduction of the closed auto was an industry first, one which its larger competitors were soon forced to adopt.[5] This success enabled the company to build a mammoth production facility at Jefferson and Conner Avenues and broaden its product offerings.

While the early postwar years were profitable for Hudson, the beginning of the 1950s saw a steep drop in sales due to reduced demand and material shortages caused by the Korean War and labor unrest. At the same time, Nash-Kelvinator began to experience some of the same issues.

By 1952, the two independent automakers' status, along with Packard and Studebaker, created an atmosphere ripe for mergers. In 1954, a merger agreement was struck between Nash-Kelvinator and Hudson Motors to form American Motors Corporation. George Mason (who was named president) worked to include Packard and Studebaker in the deal but unfortunately died before an agreement could be completed. Mason's successor was future Michigan governor George Romney.

Both Hudson and Nash-Kelvinator brought strengths to the table. The successful Nash Rambler, now a compact two-door sedan, anchored the small-car offerings, while Hudson concentrated on larger cars. Eventually, the product lines were integrated, with rebadged versions of the Rambler offered through Hudson dealerships.

HUDSON SUPER SIX RACE CAR IN FRONT OF OLD EXECUTIVE BUILDING, WASHINGTON

LIBRARY OF CONGRESS

ALL-NEW, GLAMOROUS NEW JET STREAM STYLING

Rambler

Custom 4-Door Cross Country for 1958

1958 RAMBLER STATION WAGON VINTAGE AD

HIP POSTCARD

THE WHIZ KIDS AT FORD

■ **AS THE WAR CAME TO A CLOSE,** Ford Motor Company's newly minted president Henry Ford II saw how his family's company had become a shambles. Meeting wartime production needs left engineers with no new car models to introduce. An antiquated accounting department estimated expenses by weighing stacks of invoices. During the prewar era, the Ford company often promoted based on personal loyalty to Henry Ford, not necessarily competence. The deficiency of expertise had consequences; Ford lost $60 million in 1946.

During the war, Charles "Tex" Thornton, a young officer in the US Army Air Forces who possessed strong analytical and mathematical skills, was assigned to organize a new unit. It would be tasked with using newly developed statistical methods to optimize procurement and distribution of war materiel. The system proved successful, and as the war ended, Thornton and his staff decided to offer their collective expertise to the private sector.

Ford Motor Company was among the companies the team approached, offering their services only if they were hired en masse. Eager for help, Henry Ford II agreed to the group's requirements. Each person took positions in departments most commensurate with his specific skills.

Arjay Miller and J. Edward Lundy began in finance, eventually rising to become company president and chief financial officer, respectively. Ben Mills was appointed general manager of the Lincoln Mercury Division. Charles Bosworth rose to become director of purchasing, while Francis Reith turned around the fortunes of Ford of France. Robert McNamara, the group's self-appointed leader, became general manager of the Ford Division and briefly preceded Miller as company

FORD WHIZ KIDS
PUBLIC DOMAIN

president before leaving to become Secretary of Defense in the Kennedy administration.

Together with Ernest Breech (recruited by Henry Ford II from Bendix Aviation), the Whiz Kids largely succeeded in bringing Ford Motor Company into the modern age. Ironically, the team's members were not themselves "car people." Rather, they knew how to gather and extrapolate data to make it useful to the decision makers.

According to retired Ford chairman Allan Gilmour, the group instituted "profit forecasts, production scheduling, sales analyses, pricing, and facility analyses. . . . they articulated the concepts of understanding the process of decision making. What information you need, what the alternatives are. How you measure the outcomes of various alternatives in advance."[6]

THE GENERAL MOTORS TECHNICAL CENTER

■ *AS WORLD WAR II NEARED ITS END,* GM Chairman Alfred Sloan took stock of the company's research and design facilities. His assessment indicated their woeful inadequacy. Engineering, design, and advanced research operations were scattered around several Detroit locations, affecting both their efficiency and ability to coordinate.

Managers from these departments expressed their desire for a consolidated site. They felt such a facility would allow the various teams to better collaborate on future

GM STYLING DOME
LIBRARY OF CONGRESS

products, which would undoubtedly be more technologically sophisticated than their predecessors.

Senior management decided to create a suburban campus-like environment, but considerable discussion ensued regarding what architectural style to adopt. The more fiscally conservative executives wanted a group of purely functional buildings built at minimal cost, while Director of Styling Harley Earl advocated for hiring a well-known, accomplished architect to craft a refined, understated facility that would capture the spirit of a new era of hope and optimism, ideas that represented the postwar period.[7] Sloan concurred, and soon celebrated architect Eero Saarinen was awarded the commission.

By 1945, GM management had decided on a 900-acre site in what was then a rural area of Warren Township. After acquiring the land, preliminary work began in late 1945, but the project was put on hold due to strikes and competing internal priorities. Completion was delayed until 1956, but at the center's

dedication, it soon became apparent that the wait was worthwhile.

Saarinen chose the International Style for the project. A cluster of low-rise buildings devoted to engineering, advanced research, and design (noteworthy for its recognizable dome) cluster around an artificial lake accented with fountains and sculpture, while some 13,000 trees and 60,000 shrubs soften the overall appearance. Lobbies of the Research and Design buildings both feature "floating staircases."[8] Glazed brick is typical in both interiors and exteriors. In addition to Saarinen's influence, work by artists Alexander Calder, Kevin Roche, Harry Bertoia, and Marianne Strengell grace the campus.

Subsequent expansions included buildings devoted to additional engineering and administrative functions. Generally, the newer structures harmonize well with the original Saarinen buildings. Today, the GM Technical Center is recognized as a National Historic Landmark.

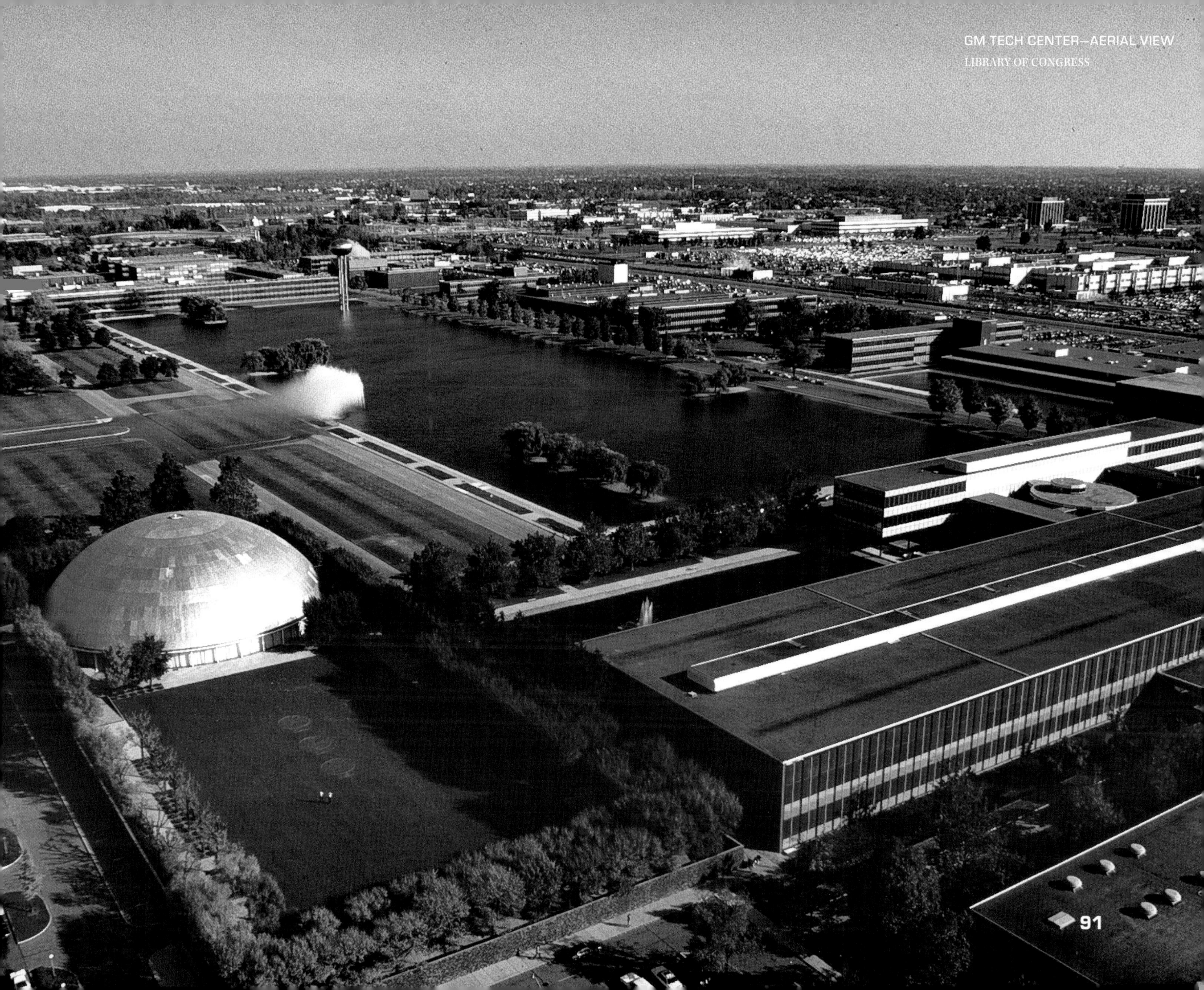

GM TECH CENTER—AERIAL VIEW
LIBRARY OF CONGRESS

GM HIRES ITS FIRST TEAM OF WOMEN DESIGNERS

■ *SINCE HARLEY EARL* first pioneered automotive design at GM, the field grew ever more sophisticated, leading the company to recruit graduates from some of the nation's top design colleges. Earl even began his own school, the Detroit Institute of Automotive Styling, which offered a correspondence course to interested prospects.

But Earl soon noticed that by the 1940s, American women were becoming more influential in a family's car purchasing decisions. Some surveys indicated as many as three out of every four sales were either made solely by or significantly impacted by women. He became convinced that women's perspectives were essential in planning and designing future products.

In 1942, Earl hired Helene Rother, a war refugee from Europe who had settled in New York. A graduate of the Kunstigwerbe in Leipzig, Germany, Rother had an impressive résumé as an independent designer of jewelry and other fashion accessories. After replying to a GM newspaper ad seeking a "designer of fashioned interiors," she applied and was hired. The sexism of the time, however, was so suffocating that senior managers insisted Rother's hiring be kept secret, fearing public embarrassment if she failed. In fact, Rother's career at GM lasted for more than four years, designing interiors for each of the company's major brands before leaving to set up her own design consulting business.

A few other women followed Rother at GM, but in 1955, a group of six female designers were hired together. Most were graduates of the prestigious Pratt Institute, a highly regarded university in Brooklyn, New York. They were known collectively as the Damsels of Design.

Four additional hires soon followed, yet only some were actually designated to design cars. Others were tasked with planning offices, while still others were assigned to the company's Frigidaire division to design kitchen appliances. Unlike the secrecy that surrounded Rother's hiring, GM promoted the group's recruitment as a marketing tool aimed at female consumers.

The original six, Marjorie Ford Pohlmann, Ruth Glennie, Jennette Linder, Sandra Longyear, Peggy Sauer, and Suzanne Vanderbilt were assigned to design interiors for Chevrolet, Buick, Cadillac, Oldsmobile, and Pontiac. Their contributions greatly enhanced the quality of their respective brands. Innovations now commonplace, including childproof doors, retractable seat belts, and storage consoles owe their origin to this team of designers. With only a few exceptions, the group's work was limited to interior work. The discriminatory customs of the day prohibited women from working on a car's exterior.

In 1957 and 1958, Harley Earl decided to showcase the team's accomplishments by staging a "Feminine Auto Show" displaying prototype models reflecting much of the team's work. GM executives from around the nation traveled to the GM Tech Center to view the exhibits in the company's famed Styling Dome.

Unfortunately, the tenures of most of the woman designers was short-lived. After Harley Earl's 1958 retirement, his successor, Bill Mitchell, proved not as accommodating. Finding their careers stymied, many went on to other design-related jobs, some outside the auto industry. Only Suzanne Vanderbilt remained past the early 1960s, retiring in 1977.

While it can be argued that GM hired the team of female designers as a publicity gimmick, the ground they broke paved the way for subsequent generations of women. Today, women are represented throughout the company and include engineers, managers, and finance people at all levels. To date, GM is the only Detroit automaker with a female CEO.

THE GM MOTORAMA

■ *THE GENERAL MOTORS CARAVAN* (later the Parade) of Progress was not the only mass publicity event of the mid-20th century at GM. From the earliest day of the industry, trade shows quickly became a customary means of marketing automobiles. The first Detroit Auto Show was held in 1899, with the New York iteration following a year later. Concurrent with the New York show, in 1931, GM president Alfred Sloan began to host an annual luncheon for industry professionals and Wall Street executives at the Waldorf Astoria Hotel. The purpose was to build trust with the financial community while displaying the company's newest models.

In 1949, the event added entertainment and displays of GM's nonautomotive technology. It was also given the name "Transportation Unlimited" and opened to the general public. The event grew and soon included domestic kitchen appliances

GM MOTORAMA 1956

furnished by GM's Frigidaire Division.[9] The national economy was enjoying a postwar boom, and the event's timing was impeccable. The 1951 and 1952 editions were canceled due to the Korean War, but in 1953, the Corvette prototype made its first public appearance.

In 1953, GM also added previously unseen concept cars, and the event was renamed "Motorama." After a nine-day run, the exhibition went on the road for the first time, and soon a caravan of tractor trailers hauled the show to Boston, Miami, Dallas, Kansas City, Los Angeles, and San Francisco. As the 1950s wore on, the show became ever more elaborate, while concept cars became more and more dominant, significantly taxing the GM design studios' staff.

By 1961, the impact of television and the beginning of more regional auto shows had reduced Motorama's audience. Meanwhile, the show became ever more costly to produce. Together, these factors led to the decision to retire Motorama.

GM MOTORAMA of 1953—Show Dates

New York, January 17-23   San Francisco, May 1-7
Miami, February 11-17   Dallas, May 16-24
Los Angeles, April 11-19   Kansas City, June 6-14

GM MOTORAMA 1953 WITH
SHOW DATES

HIP POSTCARD

CHEVY INTRODUCES THE CORVETTE

■ **WHILE AMERICAN GIs WERE FIGHTING** the war in Europe, many took note of the MGs, Jaguars, and Alfa Romeos—cars unlike anything they were accustomed to. Automakers soon picked up on their interest in these stylish "sporting" cars. At GM, design chief Harley Earl was also a fan. Soon, he and Chevrolet brand manager Thomas Keating lobbied senior GM management to add a new model to their lineup. The idea would serve two purposes: capitalizing on this emerging market while spicing up Chevy's staid image.

After receiving approval in 1952, engineers went to work in secret on Project Opel to develop an American sports car. The result was a silhouette that mimicked some of its

European rivals but sported a fiberglass body and a 235-cubic-inch straight six-cylinder engine. But much to the disappointment of would-be buyers, the car only had a two-speed automatic transmission. Recalling the Corvette, a small submarine used by the US Navy during the war, planners adopted the name for the new car.

The hand-built prototype, identified as EX-122, first went on display in January 1953 at GM's Motorama in New York. Unlike most concept vehicles on display, the Corvette entered production midway through the 1953 model year. Meanwhile, Ford's introduction of its two-seater Thunderbird underscored the importance of this new market.

The Corvette was far from an instant hit. Of the initial run of 300 cars, only 183 were sold. The weak initial sales (which may have

resulted from the high $3,450 price) almost led to the project's cancellation. But within a year, the company hired Zora Arkus-Duntov, a Belgian-born engineer and race car driver, to reimagine the car's engine and drivetrain. In 1955, a 265-cubic-inch V8 engine was offered for the first time, capable of 195 horsepower. An available three-speed manual transmission soon followed.

Over the next several years, the Corvette continued to evolve into a high-performance sports car. The first generation of the Corvette ran until 1962 before a redesign created the familiar stingray silhouette. An American automotive icon, in February 2020, the eighth generation was introduced, which included a mid-mounted engine for the first time.

CORVETTE
PIXABAY

THE DEMISE OF STUDEBAKER-PACKARD

■ *SINCE ITS FOUNDING IN 1899,* the Packard brand grew to symbolize excellence in engineering and luxury. Despite occasionally venturing into the economy car market, the company emerged from World War II with an initial desire to return to its roots—a low-volume manufacturer of luxury automobiles.

But as the 1950s dawned, Packard president James Nance wanted his company to become the cornerstone of a new, GM-like constellation of brands, ranging from entry up to premier level. To accomplish this, Packard acquired Studebaker in 1954 to form Studebaker-Packard Corporation. The plan was for each company to maintain separate lines while benefiting from each other's dealer networks.

After a period of stabilization, Nance envisioned a mega merger between his company, Hudson, and Nash-Kelvinator. Packard would occupy the top tier, followed by the others in descending order. But once Nash and Hudson merged to form American Motors, George Romney, who succeeded George Mason, refused to consider other acquisitions. Soon, management at Packard discovered that Studebaker's financial condition was much worse than they were led to believe.

Several other misfortunes befell the company. Lacking the styling resources of its larger competitors, Packard models of the 1950s often looked dated. The "high pockets" design on convertible models gave the car an exaggerated rear fender pocket but failed to draw the public's attention in the way Cadillac's rear tail fins did.[10]

Chrysler's acquisition of Briggs Manufacturing Company, which had been Packard's supplier of bodies, forced Packard to return to in-house production at considerable cost. Several attempts were made at reorganization, which called for Studebaker to play a more prominent role. In 1954, the company revived the previously used Clipper name for a new moderately priced model.

By 1957, the Studebaker influence on engineering and design had grown so strong the vehicles were derisively called "Packardbakers." The plant on East Grand Boulevard was closed, and production was relocated to the Studebaker factory in South Bend, Indiana. The last Packards rolled off the line in 1959, and the company reverted to the Studebaker name in 1962. Studebaker continued until 1966, when the company dissolved.

EMPLOYEES STANDING IN FRONT OF
PACKARD PLANT, 1956

WALTER P. REUTHER LIBRARY, ARCHIVES OF URBAN
AND LABOR AFFAIRS, WAYNE STATE UNIVERSITY

1935 STUDEBAKER

CONSTRUCTION OF DETROIT'S EXPRESSWAYS—INFLUENCE OF THE AUTO INDUSTRY

■ **WHILE THE ASCENT** of the auto industry affected every corner of the globe, its impact on the city of Detroit appeared to be outsized. And while every major US city built expressways during the postwar years, few places matched the density of Detroit's network of high speed, limited access roads.

Tracing the ever-changing footprint of the industry offers some explanation. By the 1950s, many of the big three's legacy facilities had become old and outdated, requiring replacement. Simultaneously, architects and plant engineers determined that modern auto plants should be constructed as single-story buildings to maximize productivity. Assembling the land needed for these new mammoth factories proved impossible with Detroit's city limits, necessitating suburban locations. And auto workers needed a quick, efficient way of getting there.

Auto executives were offered a glimpse of this new model during World War II. The Detroit Industrial Freeway (aka "Bomber Road") was built for workers from Detroit to get to the Ford Willow Run plant in Ypsilanti to build the B-24 bomber. The road was later integrated into the Interstate Highway System as I-94. Convinced of its effectiveness, the automakers vigorously pursued this strategy. After World War II, virtually every new auto-related facility was built outside the city limits.

This trend came at the expense of the city's public transit system. With many of the new destinations outside the area serviced by Detroit's streetcars, ridership declined, leading to service reductions. Historian Thomas Sugrue offers an insightful observation:

> It seemed somehow appropriate that the city that had given birth to the automobile industry had one of the nation's poorest and least accessible public transit systems by the end of the twentieth century.[11]

The passage of the Interstate Highway Act of 1956 targeted federal funding toward expressway construction. Planners responded to the era's racial politics and routed the new roads through predominantly black areas while avoiding white middle-class neighborhoods. The most egregious example was the construction of the I-75, the Oakland-Hastings (now the Chrysler) Expressway. The project uprooted Paradise Valley near downtown, the center of African American entertainment and shopping, plus the adjacent Black Bottom, the community's residential district.

Viewed from today's perspective, the disadvantages of urban expressways are all too evident. Once vibrant neighborhoods became isolated, cut off from pedestrian traffic. The expressways also accelerated overall suburbanization, contributing to the economic decline of the city.

CONSTRUCTION OF FISHER FREEWAY

WALTER P. REUTHER LIBRARY, ARCHIVES OF URBAN
AND LABOR AFFAIRS, WAYNE STATE UNIVERSITY

CHRYSLER
K CAR 1
CORPORATION

CHAPTER EIGHT

THE LATE 20TH CENTURY (1960–2000)

AT THE BEGINNING of the 1960s, Detroit's Big Three automakers were at their zenith. With a 90% share of the domestic market, GM, Ford, and Chrysler sold more than 8.3 million cars and trucks in 1960.[1] Profits were bountiful, while issues of safety, emissions, fuel economy, and foreign competition were of little concern.

While this may not have been an ideal management strategy, this carefree approach was reflected in some of the industry's most notable products of the decade. The Ford Mustang, the original pony car, succeeded at capturing an emerging youth market. Other entries were an array of "muscle cars"—the Chevrolet Camaro, Dodge Challenger, and the Pontiac GTO—with massive engines and horsepower ratings north of 450. Members of the baby boomer generation were just reaching driving age, and weekend "cruising" became an enduring symbol of the 1960s. Gas remained cheap, while a robust national economy sustained this new, youth-oriented culture.

But soon the euphoria of the sixties gave way to the somber reality of the seventies. An unexpected explosion in oil prices, new concerns about safety and the environment, plus a spike in competition from abroad all combined to permanently alter the industry. The Big Three would be forced to change, and so would America.

THE CHRYSLER TURBINE

■ **TODAY, RESEARCHERS** are working on the next generation of alternative fuel vehicles, electric vehicles, and other forms of mobility, intending to wean the motoring public off the gas-powered internal-combustion engine. The reasons, of course, are concerns over the health of the environment, the finite supply of oil, and chronic urban congestion.

The overall effort, however, goes back further than most may realize. As far back as the late 1930s, researchers at Chrysler began work on turbine engines for use in aircraft. After World War II, chief engineer George Huebner led a secret team dedicated to producing a turbine for automotive use. The challenge was to take a jet aircraft engine's technology and adapt it to turning a driveshaft to deliver torque to the wheels.

Researchers believed a turbine could be more efficient and require less maintenance. Turbines were lighter, had fewer moving parts, and could run on various alternative fuels: gasoline, kerosine, even vegetable oil. After several years of effort, Chrysler achieved a key breakthrough when it developed a heat regenerator, which took the extremely hot exhaust and redirected it back to the front of the engine, where it would mix with the intake air. The result was enhanced safety and improved fuel economy.

Chrysler publicly revealed its first turbine car in June of 1954.

CHRYSLER TURBINE

Improved versions followed in 1956 and 1961. The 1961 version was successfully driven from New York City to Los Angeles. In 1963, Chrysler built 55 copies of its latest edition with an updated body style reminiscent of the Ford Thunderbird. It was no coincidence—the design was the work of newly hired designer Elwood Engel, who had previously worked at Ford.

That same year, the Chrysler turbine was tested by the public under a unique pilot program. The company built 55 cars and loaned out 50 to 203 families nationwide, each for a three-month period. In subsequent interviews, users gave generally mixed responses.[2] Participants appreciated the car's smooth ride, minimal maintenance requirements, and the ease of starting in cold temperatures. They registered complaints, however, about low fuel economy and slow acceleration. None of the cars were ever sold to the public.

When the program ended in 1966, Chrysler pronounced it a success but ultimately decided to retire the turbine.[3] Gasoline remained inexpensive, making the cost of operating a turbine car prohibitively higher than a comparatively powerful conventional vehicle.

Of the original fleet of turbines, 46 were destroyed, while the remaining nine today reside in museums and private collections. One is owned by comedian Jay Leno.

CHRYSLER TURBINE INTERIOR

GETTY IMAGES

THE 1970s OIL CRISIS

■ *BY 1973,* the industry had made early forays into the economy car sector. Yet these early compacts, such as the Ford Pinto and the Chevrolet Vega, came with significant safety and quality issues. And despite their introduction, the fuel economy of the average American car was a paltry 13 miles per gallon.[4] This was because the mainstay of the Big Three's lineup still consisted of large sedans and station wagons, many with expensive options, that guzzled gas but fueled the automakers' bottom lines.

Senior managers at each of the Big Three were largely guided by custom. Most assumed the conditions that shaped the industry's postwar prosperity would continue indefinitely. Oil would remain cheap because it had always been cheap, and the buying public would remain loyal. These executives were confident that only they understood the mind of the American consumer. Year after year of strong sales only reinforced this belief.

In June of 1973, a young oil analyst named Charley Maxwell from the Wall Street Firm Cyrus Lawrence traveled to Detroit to advise the Big Three's senior executives about an alarming discovery made in his research. Despite ridicule from many of his peers, Maxwell forecast a dramatic increase in the price of oil. He believed it would come soon and potentially have a calamitous effect on oil-dependent industries, including automobiles.

The coming spike in oil prices was, Maxwell theorized, an inevitable consequence of changes in politics of the Middle East. Most nations in the region were modernizing their societies and embracing an industrial economic model that stressed urbanization. This shift would exponentially increase their domestic need for energy. At the same time, rising Arab nationalism motivated governments to capitalize on what had until then been an undervalued natural resource.[5]

The purpose of Maxwell's trip was to make senior managers aware of the coming changes so they might plan accordingly. The reception he got was a cold one. Instead of meeting with high-level executives, those most in need of hearing his message, the analyst from New York was granted access to only low-level managers who listened politely but did little else. His warning went unheeded.

Only four months later, the cascade began. In October of 1973, OPEC, the Organization of Petroleum Exporting Countries, enacted an oil embargo on the West in response to the United States' support of Israel in the Yom Kippur War. Crude oil soon quadrupled in price. A new economic era had begun.[6]

DETROIT FREE PRESS CARTOON
JANUARY 8, 1980

DETROIT FREE PRESS

THE MALAISE ERA

■ **ACCORDING TO HISTORIAN DAVID HALBERSTAM,** a deep-seated cultural disconnect was the primary cause of the shock experienced by Detroit's auto executives in the mid-1970s. He cites David Davis, an experienced industry executive who, after studying some of the European automakers' newer innovations, noted that

"NO GAS" SIGN AT GAS STATION

WALTER P. REUTHER LIBRARY, ARCHIVES OF URBAN AND LABOR AFFAIRS, WAYNE STATE UNIVERSITY

his transatlantic competitors brainstormed potential improvements to a vehicle's safety and performance, determined their feasibility, and then strategized on the optimal way to bring them to market.

Davis could clearly see the contrast between this method and Detroit's antiquated system, one guided by a near-obsession with the "bottom line" where concerns over cost, not quality, reigned supreme. To explain this, Davis traced a decades-long shift in Detroit's way of thinking. Describing Davis's theory, Halberstam writes:

> In the old Detroit, the Detroit of car men, no one would have asked what it might cost as an option but simply whether it made the car better. . . . The new Detroit, he thought, was more cautious, a place of people who had made their way by taking as few risks as possible and never letting their eye waver from the bottom line. Innovation cost money and entailed risk, and they had little stomach for it.[7]

The virtual monopoly shared by the Big Three, rather than fostering competition, induced a complacency where, instead of innovating, each company waited for the others to try something and then steered clear of their mistake if it happened to fail.

The failure to meet the challenges of newly emerging competitors deprived the industry of effective leadership when it was needed most. The result was several model years of mediocre products that failed to meet the changing American market's needs. This period was dubbed the Malaise Era in 1979 by journalist Murilee Martin.[8] Martin dated the beginning of the Malaise Era to 1973, when the sudden spike in oil prices and the subsequent embargo caught the industry off guard. He coined the gloomy-sounding name after the pessimistic Crisis of Confidence speech delivered by President Jimmy Carter in July of 1979, which was in response to yet another oil crisis.

RALPH NADER AND AUTOMOTIVE SAFETY

■ **IN 1965, GENERAL MOTORS** engineer John DeLorean, who had achieved great success at Pontiac, was promoted to general manager of the division. But his atypical lifestyle (he preferred updated clothes and slightly longer hair and enjoyed socializing with celebrities) ruffled more than a few feathers on the 14th floor of the General Motors building.

Yet his differences with his superiors were more than superficial. After his elevation to corporate management, DeLorean was shocked to discover the cavalier way product decisions were made. Issues related to safety were too often brushed aside in deference to concerns over profit. But despite his disgust, DeLorean took a nuanced view. He personally knew the men on the committees making the decisions and felt they were fine, upstanding people. But collectively, a moral and ethical rot had taken over that often produced tragic consequences.[9]

Perhaps the most telling example was the Chevrolet Corvair's swing axle beginning in the early 1960s. The system was used to support the rear-mounted engine's weight but made the car vulnerable to flipping over, especially at higher speeds. Most notably, this design flaw was publicized in the book *Unsafe at Any Speed* by young attorney Ralph Nader.

Only the first chapter deals with the Corvair. The balance of the book evaluates other aspects of the automotive industry from the perspective of passenger safety, often with damning results. Examples include the pattern of gear arrangement on transmissions. Each manufacturer used a different arrangement, making an accident likely when a motorist familiar with one make drives the vehicle of another. He calls out stylists for using excesses of chrome on dashboards, potentially creating glare that might momentarily blind a driver.[10]

The book piqued the interest of government officials and ushered in an era of expanded safety mandates for new vehicles. The movement culminated with the creation of the National Highway Traffic Safety Administration (1966) and the US Department of Transportation (1969).

Not surprisingly, GM was not pleased. But instead of challenging Nader on the merits of the issues, it resorted to the politics of personal destruction.

Shortly after publication, the company hired a private detective firm that delved into details about Nader's personal life for incriminating information, placed threatening phone calls to his home, and even tried to entrap the author in compromising situations. In 1966, US Senator Abraham Ribicoff (D-Connecticut) held a public hearing where GM President James Roche was forced to apologize publicly.

But the consumer advocate's concerns stood the test of time. In his memoir, *On a Clear Day You Can See General Motors*, John DeLorean acknowledges that Nader's criticism was, in fact, valid.[11]

RALPH NADER
LIBRARY OF CONGRESS

THE ERA OF COLORFUL EXECUTIVES

■ **THROUGHOUT MUCH OF DETROIT'S AUTO HISTORY,** but especially during the early postwar years, the industry's top executives' uber-cautious business philosophy was reflected in an outward appearance equally restrained. These men (there were no women and few minorities among their ranks) were noted for their strongly conservative, almost bland image. Charcoal gray or navy suits, short haircuts, and white dress shirts with traditional repp ties were the unofficial uniform.

But John DeLorean, who began his career at GM as an engineer for Pontiac in 1956 and climbed the corporate ladder, was different. His unconventional thinking was reflected in his personal style as well as his product strategy. After being promoted to chief division engineer in 1961, DeLorean facilitated Pontiac's entry into the emerging "muscle car" market.

1965 GTO
VOLO AUTO MUSEUM

The result was the legendary GTO sports car. The cryptic name is an Italian acronym standing for *Gran Turismo Omologato,* a certification that a vehicle meets standards for fuel capacity and engine size that qualifies it to enter European racing competitions. The car's success earned DeLorean a promotion to general manager of Pontiac.

JOHN DELOREAN, 1982
WALTER P. REUTHER LIBRARY,
ARCHIVES OF URBAN
AND LABOR AFFAIRS, WAYNE
STATE UNIVERSITY

At Ford, a young executive named Lee Iacocca experienced similar success. Like DeLorean, Iacocca had a background in engineering. After graduating from Lehigh University and Princeton University, the Allentown, Pennsylvania, native was hired by Ford in 1946.

Switching from engineering to sales shortly after his arrival, Iacocca distinguished himself through a series of innovative ideas, including his "56 for '56" campaign, which offered prospective buyers loans for

1965 FORD MUSTANG
VOLO AUTO MUSEUM

20% down and $56 payment per month for three years.[12] The idea's success led to Iacocca's ascent through the ranks, and, by 1960, he was appointed general manager of the Ford division.

His new position gave him the ability to spearhead a new car aimed at the emerging youth market. The Mustang, introduced at the New York World's Fair in April 1964, was an instant hit. For the first year, the car was offered in both convertible and hardtop editions. Sales exceeded 559,000 units.[13]

In 1970, Iacocca was promoted to president of Ford Motor Company, but once in the position, he often clashed with Chairman and CEO Henry Ford II. In 1975, Ford nixed a deal Iacocca was working on with Honda where the two companies would share components. "No car with my name on it will ever have a Jap engine," he was quoted as saying.[14]

Eventually, Iacocca was passed over for the chance to succeed Ford as CEO, in favor of rival executive Philip Caldwell. On July 13, 1978, Henry Ford II fired Lee Iacocca. According to Iacocca, the reason Ford gave was, "Sometimes you just don't like someone."[15]

LEE IACOCCA ON
NEWSWEEK COVER
APRIL, 20 1964

Newsweek

APRIL 20, 1964 30c

THE MUSTANG:
Newest Breed
Out of
Detroit

Ford's Lee Iacocca

1968 FORD MUSTANG

HIP POSTCARD

THE SAGA OF CHRYSLER

■ *IN HIS BOOK* Riding the Roller Coaster, historian Charles Hyde chronicles almost a century of ups and downs at Detroit's third-largest automaker. In the decades since Walter Chrysler brought together Chalmers, Maxwell, and eventually Dodge into his eponymous company, Chrysler had been responsible for some of the industry's most remarkable engineering breakthroughs and had made invaluable contributions to the nation's war efforts. The company has also seen appalling strategic failures, remarkable recoveries, and the buying out of a competitor, and had itself been the subject of two buyouts by foreign concerns—not to mention several name changes. No other Detroit automaker has experienced such a tumultuous past.

During the 1960s, under Chairman Lynn Townsend, Chrysler made a series of strategic errors. When consumer preferences began to shift toward smaller vehicles, Ford and Chevrolet introduced the Maverick and Vega, respectively. Yet Chrysler continued to produce behemoths. Significant losses in 1969 prompted Townsend to slash spending on new product development, hampering Chrysler's ability to compete going forward. An ill-fated venture into real estate development (too unrelated to its core business) proved distracting.

Perhaps the most disastrous move was Townsend's decision to create a "sales bank"—an inventory of cars built for stock and not to fulfill dealer orders. The result was a massive backlog of unsold vehicles that eventually grew to more than 400,000.[16]

When the 1970s arrived, Chrysler experienced more difficulty adjusting to the new market realities than its competitors. Following the 1973–74 Arab oil embargo, the spike in oil prices increased the demand for smaller cars. Yet the Dodge Omni and Plymouth Horizon, Chrysler's first major subcompact offerings, would not be introduced until 1978. After Townsend retired in 1975, his successor, John Riccardo (who, like Townsend, had a background in accounting and not engineering), continued many of the same policies.

1964 CHRYSLER NEWPORT
HIP POSTCARD

By 1978, Chrysler was awash in red ink and on the brink of bankruptcy. Realizing he needed help, on November 2, Riccardo announced the hiring of Lee Iacocca, recently fired from Ford, as company president. The newcomer quickly went to work, replacing most senior managers (many with previous colleagues from Ford), improving internal financial controls, overhauling purchasing procedures, improving quality, and adopting a new marketing strategy.[17]

But Chrysler's situation had grown so dire that these steps were only a start. Help from the US government was seen as the only way to ensure Chrysler's survival. But the Carter administration was unwilling to assist as long as Riccardo remained CEO.[18]

After Riccardo tendered his resignation in September 1979, Iacocca was named his successor. Over the next year, Iacocca's team and Doug Fraser, president of the United Auto Workers, lobbied Congress and the White House for some form of federal assistance.

What emerged was the Chrysler Loan Guarantee Act, signed by President Jimmy Carter on January 6, 1980. The legislation outlined an elaborate plan of $1.5 billion in federally , guaranteed loans, contingent on the company's negotiation of labor concessions and price breaks from suppliers, internal cost savings, and the introduction of fuel-efficient vehicles. Ultimately, the strategy worked. By June of 1983, Chrysler had returned to profitability and paid off the last of the government-backed loans—seven years early.

WORKERS LEAVING DODGE MAIN,1970s

WALTER P. REUTHER LIBRARY, ARCHIVES OF URBAN AND LABOR AFFAIRS, WAYNE STATE UNIVERSITY

EMERGENCE OF FOREIGN COMPETITION

■ *BY THE 1950s,* Japan's industrial infrastructure had begun to emerge from the devastation of World War II. After the resurgence of its steel industry, automaking seemed a logical next step. Most postwar cars in Japan were designed for the Japanese market: small and built for economy, as most trips were short and took place in urban areas. Competition between Japanese automakers, like between all manufacturers, was intense, particularly between Nissan and Honda. Over the following years, the Japanese slowly improved and refined their manufacturing processes, always making product quality their highest priority.

To accomplish this, teams of researchers traveled to the United States and observed American auto plants, taking meticulous notes of the steps they used and didn't use. The visitors took what they learned and integrated it with the statistical control methods introduced to them by W. Edwards Deming, an American expert on quality control. According to author David Halberstam, Deming's system "provided them [the Japanese] with a series of industrial disciplines mathematically defined,

ABANDONED FACTORY
LIBRARY OF CONGRESS

and with a manner of group participation that fitted well with the traditions of their culture. It was, in essence, a mathematical means of controlling the level of quality on an industrial line by seeking ever finer manufacturing tolerances."[19]

This disciplined approach soon permeated the entire production process through planning, engineering, designing, and production. Over time, the method allowed Japan to overcome its stigma of inferior products.

Japanese automakers took advantage of liberal American trade policies and, by the early 1960s, began to market their cars in the United States. At first, the phenomenon was so minor it barely registered on the radar screen. But by the 1970s, American consumers increasingly turned to imports, citing their superior quality and fuel economy. In 1977, US sales of foreign cars exceeded two million units.

As imports became a national economic and political issue (and to save on transportation costs), foreign automakers began to build factories in the United States. In 1978, Volkswagen opened its first US plant in Westmoreland, Pennsylvania. Honda became the first Japanese carmaker to do so in 1982 when it inaugurated a facility in Marysville, Ohio.

The impact on the Big Three's market share was enormous, but the situation has stabilized in recent years. In the spring of 2020, GM, Ford, and Fiat Chrysler had a combined share of approximately 50% of the domestic market (with GM and Ford still ranking at the top, with 17.4% and 14.5%, respectively).[20] This stands in sharp contrast, however, to the 85% they enjoyed in 1961.[21]

One response by the US automakers was to acquire interests in some of their foreign counterparts. GM purchased Swedish manufacturer Saab in 1990, while Ford bought Volvo, Jaguar, Aston Martin, and Land Rover in the late 1990s.

Meanwhile, foreign carmakers continued to invest in US-based factories. None, however, were located in Michigan. BMW constructed a plant in Spartanburg, South Carolina, to build sport utility vehicles while Daimler-Benz did so in Tuscaloosa, Alabama. Korean automakers Hyundai and Kia built facilities in Montgomery, Alabama, and West Point, Georgia, respectively. And in 1998, Daimler-Benz entered into what was termed a merger of equals with Chrysler, but unexpected difficulties, due in part to cultural differences, would doom the marriage after only a few years.

CHAPTER NINE

THE 21ST CENTURY

WHEN DETROIT'S AUTO INDUSTRY reached the 21st-century threshold, it was the approximate centennial of its organization. Over the course of a century, it could boast a legacy of incredible success, patriotic engagement, consolidation, and tragic decline, the latter brought on by numerous factors—foreign competition, changing economic circumstances, and internal mismanagement.

Events of the early 1990s presaged things to come. A recession in 1990–91, caused mainly by the spike in oil prices following the Iraqi invasion of Kuwait, led to a 12% drop in domestic sales and losses at each of the Big Three. While the recession was mild compared to earlier downturns, it was followed by a sluggish recovery that produced few jobs and only modest sales growth. The following years were especially tough for GM, which flirted with bankruptcy in 1992.

The end of the decade saw a recovery when US sales hit a record 12.5 million units in 2000.[1] Sadly, however, prosperity was short-lived, and the worst was still to come.

THE 9/11 ATTACKS AND THEIR IMPACT

■ *THE TERRORIST ATTACKS* of September 11, 2001, sent the nation into economic freefall, producing a period of turbulence for the auto industry. Oil prices again began to spike, and, within the next few years, sales of large pickups, SUVs, and luxury sedans (which carried the highest profit margins) declined at each of the Big Three. By February of 2005, GM was experiencing declining profits and had accumulated a backlog of 1.3 million unsold cars.[2]

Ford's product line was viewed as uncompetitive. Toyota had just passed the company for the number two spot in domestic market share while its earnings were also eroding. Chrysler, buoyed by the fortunes of its parent company in Germany, was fairing somewhat better. These misfortunes precipitated a dip in the value of GM and Ford stock. Both companies were also struggling with soaring employee health-care costs and unrelenting foreign competition.

Over the next several years, each of the Big Three would reinvent itself. Each would embark on strenuous restructuring plans, including plant closings, layoffs, and negotiations with the United Auto Workers for wage and benefit concessions. Still, it would not be enough.

9/11 MEMORIAL

LIBRARY OF CONGRESS

THE GREAT RECESSION AND THE NEAR COLLAPSE OF THE INDUSTRY

■ **BY 2007, THE INDUSTRY** had made progress toward recovery. The labor costs gap with the overseas "transplant" manufacturers (domestic plants of foreign automakers) had largely been eliminated. The Big Three jointly set up a Voluntary Employees Beneficiary Association (VEBA) plan with the UAW to cover employee health-care costs.

But soon, the worldwide financial crisis of 2006 to 2008 gave way to what came to be known as the Great Recession. Ballooning unemployment translated into declining sales, draining the cash reserves of each of the Big Three. Losses at each of the domestic automakers continued to mount, and by April 2008, gas prices were close to $4 per gallon.

What had once been unimaginable became a reality when GM, Ford, and Chrysler were forced to ask collectively for a rescue by the US government.

In late 2008, the CEOs of each of the Big Three and the president of the UAW

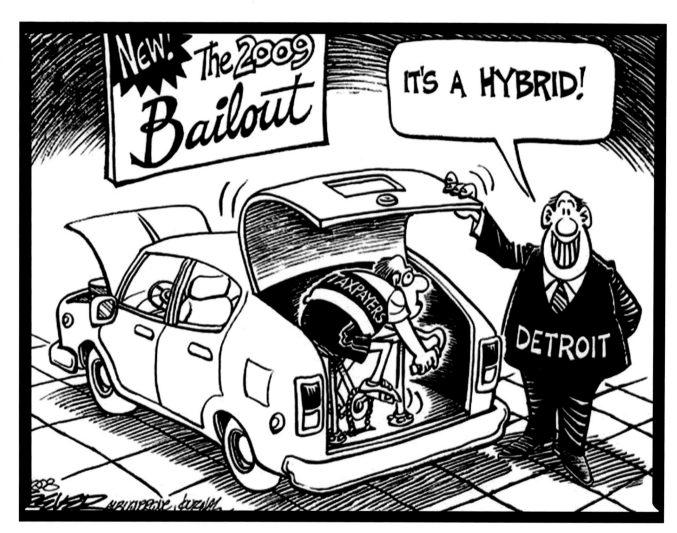

CARTOON C. 2009

THE ATLANTIC

testified before the US Senate Banking Committee requesting $34 billion in government loans to avoid Chapter 11 bankruptcy filings. In their testimony, four officials—Rick Wagoner (GM), Alan Mulally (Ford), Robert Nardelli (Chrysler), and Ron Gettelfinger (UAW)—cited a Goldman Sachs analysis that estimated a $1 trillion impact on the US economy if the industry were to collapse. Even if only one automaker were forced to liquidate, the negative effect on the supplier network would seriously jeopardize the other two since most vendors did business with two or more of the Big Three.[3]

A partial lifeline had come the previous September when Congress authorized a $25 billion loan to stave off bankruptcy. In December, President George W. Bush approved an additional $17.4 billion loan, drawn from the Troubled Assets Relief Program (TARP; a figure that would ultimately grow to more than $50 billion, for which the government would take 912 million GM shares, a 60.8% stake in the company). This loan would be disbursed by the incoming Obama administration. As preconditions, the automakers were required to submit to federal oversight, impose stringent new cost-cutting measures, and extract more concessions from the UAW.

But even these resources were not enough. After the US government turned down GM and Chrysler's requests for additional funds, what was once unthinkable happened. On April 30, 2009, Chrysler LLC filed for Chapter 11 bankruptcy. GM followed on June 1.

Both companies followed a debt-relief path during their bankruptcies and used the aid to stabilize their operations. The federal government also became a major stockholder in GM while requiring that Rick Wagoner step down. Chrysler was required to find a merger partner.

The draconian measures proved to be the remedy the beleaguered industry needed. Chrysler soon merged with Italian automaker Fiat SpA, while GM emerged from Chapter 11 in a mere 40 days. Ford accepted no government aid and avoided bankruptcy, but still had a vital stake in GM and Chrysler's fates. Due to the industry's synergies (sharing parts suppliers and drawing from the same pool of skilled tradespeople), Ford's survival was tethered to that of its crosstown rivals.

TIME COVER 2/16/2009
PUBLIC DOMAIN

INDUSTRY LEADERS TESTIFYING
BEFORE CONGRESS
GETTY IMAGES

IMPACT ON THE CITY OF DETROIT

■ *IN WHAT IS PERHAPS AMONG THE GREATEST IRONIES* in American history, the industrial concern most responsible for Detroit's remarkable growth eventually became central to its decline.

At the dawn of the 20th century, when Detroit's earliest automotive entrepreneurs set up their shops, the need for a better means of mobility was obvious. Although other heavy industries emerged from the Second Industrial Revolution, transporting goods and people over land was limited to the horse and buggy or along the railroad lines' arbitrary paths.

At first a novelty, automobiles soon captured the public imagination. When Henry Ford introduced the first mass-produced cars aimed at the general public, the resulting boom was epochal. The company sold millions. The sudden need for labor drew immigrants and transplants from the American South in droves, swelling Detroit's population from just 285,000 in 1900 to almost one million within 20 years. The auto industry's role in producing military hardware during World War II would draw even more newcomers. By 1950, Detroit boasted 1.8 million residents, making it the fourth-most populous US city.

But while the production of cars fueled Detroit's prosperity, the very freedom the auto provided—mobility—combined with other factors to spur the city's decline. As the population grew, residential neighborhoods were built around the city's core, expanding like rings on a tree over succeeding generations.

Racism soon reared its ugly head. Even before 1900, entrenched segregation patterns confined African Americans to a small area immediately east of downtown. The Black Bottom neighborhood (the name given to it by 18th century French farmers regarding the dark soil)

URBAN BLIGHT
PUBLIC DOMAIN

was overcrowded and unhealthy. Segregation, enforced by restrictive deed covenants and other methods, prevented full black participation in civic life.

But as the decades wore on, legions of once urban residents moved ever further out, aided by almost universal car ownership, the construction of expressways, and the availability of cheap land on the city's fringe. Businesses (including newer, more modern auto plants) joined the suburban exodus in the years following World War II. The result was a city stripped of its middle class and economic resources, causing much of the blight still in evidence today.

While Detroit was by no means the only American city that experienced these problems, significant research suggests that urban abandonment and "white flight" had their greatest impact in southeast Michigan. Can this be attributed to the area's automotive heritage? Historians will surely debate this question for years to come.

The End of Detroit, Micheline Maynard's book on the domestic auto business's troubles, may have an unintentional double meaning in its title. While the book uses the word "Detroit" as a metonym for the auto industry (a custom still popular today), the title could also serve as a reference to the urban problems affecting its namesake city.

GM REFORMS AND RECOVERS

■ **GM'S BANKRUPTCY** was followed by a period of painful reform. The Hummer and Saab brands were sold, while the Saturn subsidiary was eliminated. Staff was reduced, and plants closed. Within the following two years, the company had four CEOs. But luckily, the benefits provided by the restructuring efforts coincided with an upturn in the national economy. In the first quarter of 2010, the automakers posted a profit of $865 million. In 2010, as GM resumed selling stock to the public, the government began to gradually sell off its holdings.

By 2014, the US government recouped more than $38 billion of its GM investment, while the company realized profits of more than $22 billion. The government decided against recovering the remaining $10.6 billion, which sparked considerable controversy. GM later claimed that if it paid back the additional funds, which would have been more than what was owed under the agreed-upon restructuring plan, it risked a lawsuit from shareholders.[4]

GM HEADQUARTERS
LIBRARY OF CONGRESS

HART PLAZA
PAUL VACHON

EPILOGUE

THE PROMISE OF NEW FORMS OF MOBILITY

PREDICTING THE FUTURE is always tricky—like trying to hit a moving target. This is because we can only make prognostications based on the information we possess at a given time, and because research continuously yields new data, forecasts must be continually revised.

The arrival of the 21st century, however, has revealed one corollary. The realities of a growing population, ever-urgent environmental concerns, and an always-shifting economy will require that the concept of mobility—moving people and things from point A to point B—be thoroughly rethought. New ideas for mobility are diverse and seem limited only by the imagination. While some can involve new mass-transit applications (self-driving buses, high-speed commuter rail, etc.), others will build on the existing technology of the automobile.

At this writing, Ford Motor Company is midway through its restoration of the long-abandoned Michigan Central Station, Detroit's once-opulent railroad depot, plus an adjacent structure originally built as a mail facility for the station. Known colloquially as "Detroit's Ellis Island," Michigan Central was the point of arrival for thousands of newcomers from 1914 to 1988, many drawn to the city's bustling auto plants.

Ford envisions a revival of not just a building, but the entire historic Corktown neighborhood. The core function of the project will be as a center for research into all types of future mobility, including new generations of electric, hybrid, and other alternative-fuel vehicles. The development will also be a community gathering spot—with portions open to the public and seamlessly integrated with the surrounding blocks.

ELECTRIC

IRONICALLY, ELECTRIC POWER was one of the first power options considered and occasionally used by the earliest auto pioneers. Early examples included Andreas Flocken's Elektrowagen in Germany and Thomas Parker's first electric car in England, both in the 1880s. Locally, the Detroit Electric Company marketed a successful electric vehicle beginning in 1907. But as improvements to internal-combustion engines made that technology more appealing (ease of refueling, superior range, etc.), electric cars' popularity began to wane.

GM EV-1

■ **REGARDLESS** of economic conditions, a segment of the public has consistently maintained its interest in electric vehicles. Although continued research took place throughout the 20th century, it wasn't until the early 1990s that GM, responding to positive customer feedback for the idea, decided to manufacture and market a production electric car, the first in the contemporary era. The EV-1 made its debut in 1996 and was available for lease only to drivers in Los Angeles, California, and Phoenix and Tucson, Arizona. The car used a three-phase AC induction motor powered by lead acid batteries. The EV-1 offered a range of 55 miles on a full charge, although the second generation, equipped with a nickel hydride battery, increased this figure to 108 miles.

Between 1996 and 1999, GM produced 1,117 EV-1s. Although the car was enthusiastically received, in 2003, GM abruptly canceled the program, stating that the vehicle could not be produced and marketed profitably. The company terminated the EV-1 leases and mandated that customers return the cars, despite strong opposition from many drivers. GM's termination of the EV-1 program proved to be very controversial. It even inspired a documentary film, *Who Killed the Electric Car*, which featured several Hollywood celebrities who had leased the car, including Tom Hanks, Ed Begley Jr., and Peter Horton.

GM EV-1

CHEVY BOLT

■ *BY 2010,* GM again embraced auto electrification with the introduction of the Chevy Volt, an extended-range hybrid vehicle, followed by the like-named Chevy Bolt. This all-electric compact represents a breakthrough in electric automotive technology. After several years of research, the Bolt debuted in 2016 at the Consumer Electronics Show in Las Vegas. The first generation ran on a lithium-ion battery capable of producing 60 kWh, which delivered a range of some 240 miles, a new benchmark for electric vehicles.

CHEVY BOLT
SPARE-WHEEL.COM

MUSTANG MACH-E
AUTOBLOG.COM

FORD MUSTANG MACH-E

■ *SINCE THE 1990s,* electric vehicle technology has made considerable breakthroughs. In 2020, Ford introduced the Mustang Mach-E, a crossover style, electric version of the automaker's long popular "pony" car. Available in variants with different capabilities, the extended range Mach-E offers an output of 88 kWh, yielding 290 horsepower, and can deliver a range of some 300 miles. Intended as both a production vehicle and a "test bed" for evolving technologies, Ford plans to introduce more powerful editions of the Mustang Mach-E soon.

HYBRID

ONE OF THE earliest alternative propulsion methods was the hybrid car, a vehicle equipped with two power sources, an internal combustion engine and an electric motor. These two systems can work independently or in tandem, as is the case with the Chevrolet Volt. The primary advantage to a hybrid is that each power source can compensate for the other's disadvantages.

CHEVY VOLT

CHEVY VOLT

■ *YEARS AFTER* its experience with the EV-1, GM was eager to compete with the Toyota Prius, the Japanese automaker's successful entry into the hybrid market. But instead of a conventional hybrid, GM decided to develop a new concept, an extended-range electric car. In all but a few driving situations, the Volt runs off a 149-horsepower electric motor powered by an 18.4 kWh lithium ion battery.[1] When the battery has a full charge, the car has a range of 53 miles, but this is extended through the use of a four-cylinder, 84-horsepower engine that turns a generator, which in turn recharges the battery. With the battery fully charged and the 12-gallon gas tank filled to capacity, the second-generation Volt could deliver a range of more than 400 miles. Over its eight-year run, GM sold more than 150,000 units of the Volt in the United States, making it one of the best-selling electric vehicles of the era, despite a price of $40,000 before government incentives. The Volt's cancellation in 2019 was due to shifts in the market. Sedans (of which the Volt was one) were falling out of favor with customers. Simultaneous technological improvements made electric-only vehicles (such as the Bolt) a more cost-effective alternative.

HYDROGEN FUEL CELLS

PERHAPS THE MOST ECO-FRIENDLY but technologically challenging alternative is the hydrogen fuel cell. With this technology, atoms of liquid hydrogen (a concentrated and therefore more efficient form of hydrogen) are directed through a channel (a positive terminal) into a chamber using a platinum catalyst. At that point, the atoms are split into hydrogen ions (protons) and electrons. The positively charged protons then cling to the negative terminal while the electrons are directed to a circuit that powers an electric motor which drives the car's wheels. The electrons are then reunited with the protons and then combined with the ambient oxygen, which triggers a chemical process that yields only water or water vapor.

Liquid hydrogen is the fuel needed to make a fuel cell work. While operating a fuel cell produces no harmful emissions, producing liquid hydrogen in an environmentally friendly way remains a considerable challenge. The process, known as electrolysis, involves using electricity to split water into hydrogen and oxygen, its two chemical components. If the electricity source is the standard electric grid, greenhouse gases remain part of the overall equation. Producing liquid hydrogen from electricity derived from wind or solar sources would be the perfect combination.

FORD AIRSTREAM
PROTOTYPE
WIKIMEDIA COMMONS

Fuel-cell vehicles face other technical hurdles. One involves engineering onboard hydrogen storage tanks that are sufficiently durable (since liquid hydrogen is highly combustible) yet light enough for the car to run efficiently. A related concern is designing the vehicle to accommodate an adequately sized tank and equipping it with a powerful enough motor to deliver a range competitive with conventional cars.

FORD PROTOTYPE
FUEL CELL CAR
GETTY IMAGES

131

AUTOMATED VEHICLES

IN 2008, the National Highway Traffic Safety Administration issued a report to Congress that cited driver error as the cause or partial cause in a full 93% of all traffic accidents.[2] While statistics can vary based on individual drivers, weather conditions, type of road, and so on, the composite role of human fallibility in crashes suggests that assistance provided by technology can improve overall safety.

Research into "automated" vehicles (the term preferred by the Society of Automotive Engineers) has been conducted for decades but has produced its most significant breakthroughs since 2000. At present, researchers envision six levels of technological capability.

The first, or Level 0, describes a vehicle similar to conventional cars but has systems capable of warning drivers of imminent obstacles or hazards.

LEVEL 1 denotes vehicles equipped with features designed to automate critical functions (such as cruise control) or perform routine but challenging tasks, such as parallel parking. Cars with both Level 0 and Level 1 capabilities are available today.

LEVEL 2 (also known as "hands off") vehicles are capable of autonomously steering, accelerating, and braking. However, these systems require constant driver attentiveness and can only function along predetermined routes.

LEVEL 3 (or "eyes off") capability performs all Level 2 functions but can also anticipate and react to changes in traffic conditions. While the driver can read or make a phone call, she must still be ready to respond to unforeseen situations.

LEVEL 4 (or "mind off") vehicles perform all essential functions seamlessly along predetermined routes, allowing the driver to fully disengage. However, if the vehicle ventures off the route, the driver must be ready to take control.

LEVEL 5 (or "steering wheel optional") vehicles represent the gold standard of autonomous motorized travel and require no driver involvement.

The introduction of these capabilities results from breakthroughs in various technologies, including radar, sonar, lidar (a device that measures distance by reflecting a laser off a target and timing its return), GPS, and odometry.

While the ongoing research is promising, the broad implementation of automated vehicles is contingent on further improvements. For example, artificially matching the acuity level of human senses requires very complex software. And since humans write software, errors can creep into the process.

Your number
8021З648
access permission

52

28

0218

THE OBSCURE "ALSO RANS" OF DETROIT AUTO LORE

EARLY IN THE 20TH century, when the American auto industry took root in Detroit, scores of aspiring investors, mechanics, and speculators saw the opportunity to build and market the amazing new invention. What many failed to anticipate was the complexity inherent in the new venture. The intricacies of financing, designing, producing, marketing, and selling a motor vehicle caused many of these early entrants to meet a quick demise. Several of these budding automakers, however, left their imprints on automotive history during their short lives.

CHALMERS-DETROIT

THE EARLY YEARS of the auto industry in Detroit resembled a lottery. While a new entrant's success was by no means assured, those who did achieve it could experience a windfall—Henry Ford being the most telling example.

In 1907, Hugh Chalmers, a manager with National Cash Register in Dayton, Ohio, was approached by businessman Roy Chapin to join Detroit-based Thomas-Detroit, a young automaker experiencing difficulties. As an enticement, the company would be renamed after Chalmers.

Although he had no automotive experience, Chalmers was assisted by Chapin and Chief Engineer Howard Coffin. The company aimed at a more affluent customer by building larger, more luxurious cars. For 1910, the 30 Roadster and the 30 Touring sold for $1,500, an exceptionally high price for the

time.[1] The models each featured a 226-cubic-inch 4-cylinder engine capable of 30 horsepower. Strong sales allowed the company to construct a mammoth factory at Jefferson and Connor Avenues.

Despite several years of success, Chapin wanted to capitalize on the small car market. Chalmers disagreed, which prompted Chapin and Coffin to join Hudson Motors, a new startup.

CHALMERS JEFFERSON PLANT
LIBRARY OF CONGRESS

In 1917, Chalmers partnered with Maxwell Motors to produce vehicles for the US military engaged in World War I. Subsequent financial problems at both companies resulted in a merger in 1922, but an economic recession caused sales to slide further. The company's creditors recruited Walter Chrysler, who had recently rescued Willys Overland, to reorganize Chalmers-Maxwell. In the process, he named the company for himself, eliminated the two legacy names, and replaced them with three brands: Plymouth, DeSoto, and Chrysler. The Dodge Brothers Company was acquired in 1928.

1912 CHALMERS
HIP POSTCARD

HUPP

■ *BY 1910,* several years of auto manufacturing in Detroit had produced the second generation of entrepreneurs—young men who were alumni of Ford, Olds Motor Works, or Buick. One was Robert "Bobby" Hupp. Equipped with a basic knowledge of the trade, in 1908, this former Ford employee partnered with investors Charles Hastings, J. Walter Drake, and Edwin Denby to establish Hupp Motor Car Company.

Its first car, the Model 20 Runabout, debuted in 1909 and was very well received; by the following year, production reached 5,000 units. It was cheap yet reliable, and the Detroit Police Department decided to purchase the 20 as its first squad car. "Hupmobiles," as they became known, were also among the first motorized vehicles used by the US military. The vehicle even earned the accolades of Henry Ford.

Robert Hupp left the business in 1913, but for the next 28 years, his namesake company introduced a succession of new models (including the 1925 introduction of an eight-cylinder engine) and emerged as a formidable competitor to Ford and Chevrolet. In the 1930s, Hupp introduced a styling revolution with the Model J Aero-Dynamic conceived by designer Raymond Loewy.

While the company weathered the Depression, by 1939, its comparatively small size caught up with it. Unable to achieve the economics of scale enjoyed by its competitors, despite a partnership with Indiana-based Graham-Paige Motor Company, Hupp Motors shut down in 1939.

REO

AFTER LEAVING the Olds Motor Works in early 1904, Ransom Olds gave every indication that he had permanently left the budding auto industry. He dabbled in a variety of different businesses, most notably real estate. But Olds could still see the enormous potential of autos, predicting they would one day replace horses. After only a few months, he began planning to reenter the business with an entirely new company.

Olds established the R. E. Olds Motor Car Company in Lansing in August of 1904. No sooner had Olds set up his new shop than Olds Motor Works sued, claiming the new business's name was too similar to theirs. Looking for a solution, Olds selected the name REO Motor Car Company (his initials).

To avoid the infighting that characterized his previous venture, Olds took a 52% ownership in the new company, giving him controlling interest. But, ironically, the first product was a heavy touring car, precisely the style Samuel and Fred Smith had championed a few years earlier that Olds had opposed. Also offered was the more economical REO Model B Runabout.

The early REO models were successful and enabled the company to expand its product line. In 1910, the REO Motor Truck Company was formed as a subsidiary and debuted the REO Model H Power Wagon the following year. At just 12 horsepower, it was seen as the forerunner to the modern pickup truck. Over the next several years, the truck line was expanded, delivering such legendary models as the REO Speed Wagon. The nameplate endured until 1953 and was produced in editions as varied as fire engines, delivery vans, and farm vehicles.

By 1922, Ransom Olds personally lost interest in REO and retired as president. Under his successor, Richard H. Scott, the company continued to prosper throughout the 1920s. When the Depression grew worse in 1933, Olds briefly emerged from retirement to assist. The company soon dropped cars in favor of trucks, the product for which REO became famous.

REO IN NEW YORK TO
SAN FRANCISCO RACE
LIBRARY OF CONGRESS

DETROIT ELECTRIC

TODAY, ENGINEERS are diligently working on new propulsion methods to wean the motoring public off the internal combustion engine. Finding this holy grail will enhance environmental quality, reduce oil dependence, and make driving more efficient. But surprisingly, the technology to accomplish this has existed for over a century.

In the industry's earliest days, little standardization existed. Methods of propulsion, the positioning of pedals, and even the side of the car with the steering wheel all varied between manufacturers. Engineers felt free to experiment.

Using an electric motor to drive a vehicle was seen as very fitting for early 20th-century driving. Many trips were short and took place in dense urban areas, where the cars' limited range was less of a disadvantage. Electric propulsion also eliminated gear shifting, offered smoother rides, and did away with exhaust fumes. Instead of an exterior crank, a simple interior switch was all that was needed to start an electric car, a plus for female drivers.

Capitalizing on this need, Anderson Electric Car Company (which later changed its name to Detroit Electric) began to offer its first cars

DETROIT ELECTRIC SERVICE STATION, CONTEMPORARY VIEW

BENJAMIN GRAVEL

DE IN WASHINGTON, D.C.
LIBRARY OF CONGRESS

in 1907. Detroit Electrics were served by a series of charging garages strategically located throughout the city. Amazingly, one of these buildings survives today on East Grand Boulevard near Jefferson Avenue. After the days of Detroit Electric, the building served as a Buick showroom and as a stage for producing industrial films. Today, it houses an art studio.

Detroit Electrics were popular with many prominent citizens, including Clara Ford, spouse of Henry Ford. In 1914, Henry purchased a Model 47 brougham for his wife.

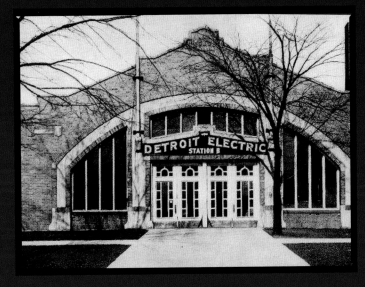

DETROIT ELECTRIC SERVICE
STATION, PERIOD VIEW

BENJAMIN GRAVEL

VINTAGE AD

KAISER CAR

WALTER P. REUTHER LIBRARY,
ARCHIVES OF URBAN AND LABOR
AFFAIRS, WAYNE STATE UNIVERSITY

KAISER-FRAZER

■ **ONE OF THE VERY FEW** automakers that began after World War II, Kaiser-Frazer emerged through the combined efforts of Joseph W. Frazer, a seasoned automotive executive, and businessman Henry J. Kaiser. Frazer had held a variety of positions at Chrysler, Willys-Overland, and Graham-Paige. Kaiser was an industrialist who invested in fields as varied as shipbuilding, aluminum and steel, and health care (Kaiser Permanente remains a major health-care provider today).

As World War II drew to a close, Frazer, who was then president of Graham-Paige, wanted to transition the company back to civilian auto production. Like executives at the Big Three, he sensed the public's pent up demand for new cars and saw an opportunity. Working to arrange financing, he met Kaiser and formed Kaiser-Frazer in partnership with Graham-Paige in 1945. In 1947, the duo purchased the assets of Graham-Paige.

Kaiser-Frazer purchased the former B-24 factory at Willow Run for its production facility. After the war, Ford Motor Company had passed on the option to acquire the plant. Although Ford had built and operated the facility, it was owned by the US government.

At first, the company marketed two principle products, each named after one of its founders. Both were sports cars, with the Kaiser being the entry-level model and the Frazer being more upscale. These were followed by the Manhattan sedan and the Vagabond hatchback. In 1953, the company introduced the Darrin, a fiberglass-bodied sports car that debuted one month before the Chevy Corvette.

Sales were brisk at first, since the Big Three offerings during the early postwar years were only slightly modified versions of their 1940–41 models. When the competition introduced all-new products by 1949, Kaiser-Frazer's sales began to ebb. Disagreements between the pair developed, causing Frazer's departure in 1951. After continuing as Kaiser Motors for a few years, Henry Kaiser engineered the purchase of Willys-Overland in 1953 and consolidated operations as Kaiser-Willys.

The company exited the passenger car market, and it was renamed Kaiser-Jeep Corporation in 1963. In 1970, it was acquired by American Motors.

RETIRED BRANDS

AN AUTOMOBILE HAS SEVERAL IDENTITIES: the manufacturer who produces it and its specific model name; think Ford Mustang or Chrysler Sebring. But in between these two identifiers, a third classification or "brand" also exists. These categories enable an automaker to group together models aimed at a particular consumer, usually identified by economic means. This concept survives, exemplified by GM's Chevrolet, Buick, and Cadillac lines.

But throughout Detroit's auto history, several brands have been retired, including some that once commanded strong customer loyalty. The reason usually reflects a change in the automaker's business strategy. Some brands slipped into obscurity, while others remain fondly remembered today. What follows is a list of influential Detroit auto brands of yesteryear.

GENERAL MOTORS

IN HIS EARLY YEARS as president of General Motors, Alfred Sloan developed a multi-tiered branding strategy. Starting with Chevrolet, each ascending brand would cater to customers of ever greater means, ending with Cadillac as the premier nameplate. As time went on, the number of brands was increased under the General Motors Companion Make Program. Under the initiative, each of the original brands was matched with an accompanying line one level below. The intention was to fill in gaps, allowing all price points to be covered.

LA SALLE

■ **THE STRATEGY** of the companion make program paired Cadillac, GM's premium make, with LaSalle, the first GM design project undertaken by longtime designer Harley Earl. Over its 13-year run (1927–1940), LaSalle produced roadster, coupe, and sedan style vehicles. They shared many of the luxury touches Cadillac was known for, but most were smaller and featured a sporty flair. Fittingly, the company named both brands for French explorers— Antoine de la Mothe, Sieur de Cadillac (Detroit's founder), and René-Robert Cavelier, Sieur de LaSalle. The latter launched a 1682 expedition that charted the Mississippi River's path from the mouth of the Illinois to the Gulf of Mexico.

VIKING

■ **ANOTHER ENTRY** in GM's companion make program, Viking, was produced from 1929 through 1931 and was attached to the Oldsmobile division. Unlike the other brands in the program, Viking was priced slightly higher than vehicles of its "parent" nameplate. It was offered as a four-door sedan, closed-coupe four-door sedan, and a deluxe convertible coupe. The Viking pioneered the monobloc V8 engine design, which featured an L-shaped combustion chamber and a horizontal valve layout capable of producing 81 horsepower.

MARQUETTE

■ **IN 1930,** GM revived the defunct Marquette brand, which had been the name of a previous company formed by William Durant in 1911. Unlike LaSalle, the new Marquette lasted only a single model year, in which it produced 35,007 vehicles. Despite its brief life, Marquette offered six different models: two sedans, two coupes, a roadster, and a phaeton.

OAKLAND

■ **THE OAKLAND** Motor Car Company was established in Pontiac, Michigan, in 1907 by Alanson Brush as a maker of simple, two-cylinder runabout autos. After being purchased by GM founder William C. Durant in 1909, Oakland was organized as the new conglomerate's entry-level division, as Chevrolet was yet to be acquired. Under GM, in 1910, Oakland introduced the Series 40, a four-cylinder touring sedan aimed at competing with Ford's Model T. In 1926, the newly created Pontiac brand was mated to Oakland under the companion make program. But in a unique move in 1931, GM retired the divisional brand (Oakland) instead of Pontiac and renamed the corporate division.

OLDSMOBILE

■ **BOTH BEFORE AND AFTER** Ransom Olds left Olds Motor Works in 1904, the company experienced success with the famous Curved Dash runabout. Originally known as "Olds automobiles," the colloquial name "Oldsmobile" soon gained currency and was celebrated in the 1905 song "In My Merry Oldsmobile." GM acquired the company in 1908, after which the brand enjoyed a storied 94-year run, producing such classics as the 1934 Oldsmobile 8 convertible, the 1957 Starfire 98 sedan, and the iconic Toronado from 1966 to 1992. By the late 1990s, however, Oldsmobile sales had begun to decline, and in December 2000, GM announced its decision to phase out the division. On April 29, 2004, the last production Oldsmobile, an Alero compact, rolled off the assembly line at the Oldsmobile plant in Lansing.

PONTIAC

■ **PONTIAC** was first introduced in 1926 by GM and mated with Oakland under its companion make program. Pontiac cars occupied a quality and performance level below Oakland during its early years and were priced accordingly. But before long, Pontiac began to outsell its sister brand, leading to the Oakland nameplate discontinuation in 1933.

Until the early 1950s, Pontiacs were marketed as traditional sedans, coupes, and station wagons. The standard engine was the straight eight-cylinder, which was replaced by a V8 in 1954. Pontiac was subsequently branded as GM's performance division, and over the next several decades, it produced some of the company's most historic cars. In 1956, John DeLorean, the division's new head of engineering, introduced the Bonneville, with one of Pontiac's first fuel injected-engines. Other classics included the Firebird sports car, the Grand Prix luxury sedan, and the GTO (Italian for Gran Turismo Omologato), one of the first "muscle cars." The first generation (1964-67) offered a 400-cubic-inch V8 rated at 325 horsepower.

Unfortunately, Pontiac met a fate similar to Oldsmobile. Declining sales and financial problems at the corporate level prompted GM to retire the brand in 2009. The very last Pontiac, a white G6 sedan, was built in January 2010 at the GM plant in Orion Township.

SATURN

■ **IN 1983,** GM Chairman Roger Smith proposed that the company design, manufacture, and market an entirely new line of cars. The strategy was that by completely rethinking the entire process, a cultural change could be effected. Many of the industry's entrenched inefficiencies could be eliminated, resulting in a product of quality design, sold and serviced through a dealer network offering the very best service. Saturn, as it was named, was intended to compete with imports by emulating their business model. It adopted the slogan "a different kind of car company."

To realize this "clean slate" concept, the new vehicle would be produced within an entirely new corporate structure, in a new factory, and sold through a new dealer network. It was a bold idea in which GM ultimately invested more than $5 billion.

After several years of product design and plant construction, the first Saturn was produced in July of 1990. The first model was the S Series compact sedan and coupe. Engineered on the Z-body frame, known as a spaceframe, the car's innovative design relieved its side panels from supporting the load. This quality allowed the panels to be constructed from lighter weight plastic, delivering better fuel economy.

Over the next several model years, various additional models were released, including the L Series mid-size sedan

and station wagon, the RELAY minivan, and the Outlook full-size crossover. Saturn even produced an eye-appealing sportscar, the Sky.

While the Saturn concept was well received by the buying public, the brand failed to provide serious competition to the imports. Sales never exceeded 300,000 units per year, or 2% of the US market.[2] Moreover, a large percentage of Saturn buyers were previous owners of other GM vehicles, not imports. Beginning in 2008, GM made an effort to sell the Saturn subsidiary. A deal struck with businessman Roger Penske called for GM to continue to produce Saturns for an additional two model years, after which Penske would need to secure another manufacturer. However, no other automaker was willing to step forward, causing Penske to withdraw from the deal. In 2010, GM decided to close the Saturn brand.

CHRYSLER

LIKE GM, Chrysler also sought to establish a hierarchy of automotive brands aimed at buyers of different economic means. While the strategy appeared well thought out, overlaps between brands with similar price points ultimately led to confusion among customers.

DESOTO

AS WALTER CHRYSLER ASSEMBLED his new car company during the 1920s, he envisioned his eponymous brand as his top-tier product. But he was acutely aware of the more cost-conscious customer who often bought Hudson or Oldsmobile. To meet this need, he introduced the DeSoto line in 1928, named after the Spanish explorer Hernando de Soto. Later that year, Chrysler also purchased the Dodge Brothers company.

To avoid redundancy, the new Dodge brand was priced slightly below DeSoto. The strategy was reversed in 1933 when Dodge assumed the middle ranking. After World War II, the DeSoto brand was revived and included models such as the full-size Firesweep, Firedome, and Fireflite during the 1950s, the latter being the brand's flagship model. The cars were known for their updated grill designs and early examples of tail fins, a feature closely identified with the era.

At the same time, however, Chrysler's customer base began to experience confusion between what seemed to be overlapping brands (Plymouth, DeSoto, Dodge, Chrysler, and Imperial, the company's highest-end offerings), leading to unwanted intracompany competition. By 1960, DeSotos began to closely resemble products from the Chrysler line. Moreover, some dealers wanted to carry some lines but not others, and some wanted to carry only one. All these factors led to the corporation's decision to terminate the DeSoto brand in 1961.

PLYMOUTH

CHRYSLER created the Plymouth brand for the most bargain-minded driver, intended to compete directly with Chevrolet and Ford. Although the early Plymouth logo sported a figure of the Mayflower, the brand drew its inspiration from the Plymouth Cordage Company, a manufacturer of twine located in Plymouth, Massachusetts.

The very first Plymouths in 1928 closely resembled Maxwell designs that Walter Chrysler inherited when he acquired the Maxwell-Chalmers Company. Intended as an economy version of a Chrysler, a Maxwell four-cylinder was rebadged as the Chrysler 52, the Chrysler-Plymouth Model Q, and finally the Plymouth Model U.

Throughout the Great Depression of the 1930s, the Plymouth's affordable cars proved to be Chrysler's bread and butter and joined Chevrolet and Ford as members of Detroit's "low-priced three" due to its reputation for value.[3]

Although Plymouth marketed an array of family cars, the brand was also represented among the muscle cars of the 1960s. By late in the decade, while Chrysler's competitors were adding more luxurious features to their muscle cars, the Plymouth Road Runner was introduced as a lower priced alternative.

The 1980s saw Plymouth play a role in Chrysler's resurgence under Lee Iacocca, with the Voyager minivan and the Reliant K-Car coupe. By 2000, however, declining sales and redundancy with other Chrysler products (many Plymouths were merely stripped down Chryslers) prompted the company to eliminate the Plymouth nameplate.

FORD

EDSEL

IN THE MID-1950S, Ford also decided to create a new brand to occupy a niche between the more economical Ford division cars and their more expensive Lincoln-Mercury counterparts. After what the company claimed was exhaustive market research, the Edsel line was introduced on September 7, 1957. Models included the entry-level Pacer and Ranger sedans, the higher-end Corsair and Citation, and three station wagons—the Roundup, the Villager, and the Bermuda. To promote the new brand, Ford hosted a TV special, *The Edsel Show*, broadcast on October 13, 1957. The live event featured luminaries such as Frank Sinatra, Rosemary Clooney, Louis Armstrong, and Bob Hope.

Ford touted the Edsel as an entirely new type of car, although some models shared engineering features with various Ford and Mercury models. However, the Edsels sported several new styling features that were used in the car's marketing. Examples included the Teletouch gear shifter (a series of buttons located on the steering wheel's hub), a rotating dome style speedometer, and the now recognizable "horse collar" grill.

But despite all the hype, sales were atrocious. Over its three-year life, only about 116,000 units were sold, far too few for the company to recoup its investment. Critics cited low quality and problems created by the design. For example, the Teletouch was placed where the horn is typically located, causing drivers to inadvertently shift gear when intending to blow the horn. The trademark grill was derided as making the Edsel look like "an Oldsmobile sucking on a lemon."

In 1960, Ford Motor Company shuttered the Edsel brand. The car's lack of success was so historic that today, the word "Edsel" is often used as a metonym for failure.

EDSEL GRILL

LIBRARY OF CONGRESS

MERCURY

■ **DURING THE 1930S,** Edsel Ford, then president of Ford Motor Company, observed multitiered model lineups adopted by his competitors. Like GM and Chrysler, Ford saw an opportunity in attracting the buyer of moderate means by offering a line of vehicles between the entry-level Ford division and the upscale Lincoln brand.

The first Mercuries resembled their intracompany counterparts except in size. Mercury models featured a 116-inch wheelbase, compared to 112 inches for Ford and 122 inches for Lincoln. The standard 239-cubic-inch flathead V8 was common to all three divisions. Although Mercury was distinct from the Lincoln brand, both were sold by a network of shared retailers, known as Mercury-Lincoln dealerships.

In 1939, the Mercury 8 was introduced and offered in sedan, coupe, and convertible configurations. Large front fenders, a peaked hood, cat-eyed headlights, and a waterfall-style grill were among the styling features. The design continued to evolve after World War II, acquiring a more streamlined look.

During the 1960s, Mercury offered several sportier models, including the Cougar, the Montego, and the Cyclone Spoiler II, a modified version of which represented Mercury on the 1969 NASCAR circuit.

By the 1970s and 1980s, Mercury's lineup was broadened to include the Mariner and Mountaineer SUVs and the Villager minivan. However, many models were almost identical to their Ford counterparts, save for a few trim differences. After 2000, Mercury sales began to decline, leading to the decision to close the brand in 2010. The Mercury-Lincoln dealerships were rebadged, while the name Lincoln Motor Company (its original moniker) was restored to the corporate division.

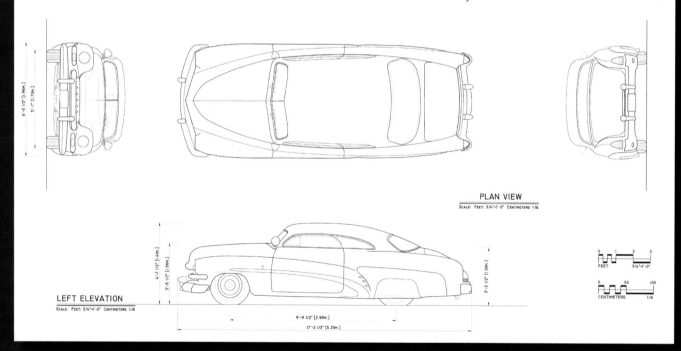

1951 MERCURY SPORT COUPE CUSTOM, HIROHATA MERC

PLAN VIEW
Scale: Feet: 3/4"=1'-0" Centimeters: 1:16

LEFT ELEVATION
Scale: Feet: 3/4"=1'-0" Centimeters: 1:16

ENDNOTES

Chapter One

1. "Railway Cars, Bricks, and Salt: The Industrial History of Southwest Detroit Before the Auto." Presentation by Thomas Klug, associate professor of history, Marygrove College, Detroit, November 3, 1999.

2. http://www.historydetroit.com/statistics/

3. Willis Dunbar and George S. May. *Michigan: A History of the Wolverine State.* Grand Rapids, Michigan: William B. Eerdmans Publishing Company, 1995, p. 412.

4. Dunbar and May, p. 413.

5. Dunbar and May, p. 414.

6. Ibid.

7. Douglas Brinkley. *Wheels for the World: Henry Ford, His Company, and a Century of Progress.* New York: Viking Press, 2003, p. 11.

8. Peter Gavrilovich and Bill McGraw. *The Detroit Almanac: 300 Years of Life in the Motor City.* Detroit: The Detroit Free Press, 2000, p. 219.

Chapter Two

1. Quentin Hardy. "Google's Horseless Carriage." *Forbes*, April 14, 2010.

2. Who Invented the Car? | Live Science. www.livescience.com/37538-who-invented-the-car.html

3. https://motorauthority.com/news/1127237_why-gas-powered-cars-aren-t-going-anywhere

4. Brinkley, p. 13.

5. Brinkley, p. 14.

6. Dunbar, p. 421.

7. George May. *A Most Unique Machine: The Michigan Origins of the American Automobile Industry.* Grand Rapids, Michigan: William B. Eerdmans Publishing Co., 1975, p. 57.

8. May, 1975, p. 59.

9. Brinkley, p. 13.

10. Brinkley, p. 14.

Chapter Three

1. G. T. Bloomfield. "Shaping the Character of a City: The Automobile and Detroit, 1900–1920." *Michigan Quarterly Review*, 25 (1986), p. 169.

2. Bloomfield, pp. 169-170.

3. *Detroit News*, August 13, 1896; quoted in May, 1975, p. 60.

4. Glenn Alan Niemeyer. *The Automotive Career of Ransom E. Olds.* Grand Rapids, Michigan: William B. Eerdmans Publishing Company, 1977, pp. 27–28; cited in May, 1975, p. 71.

5. George May. *R.E. Olds: Auto Industry Pioneer.* Grand Rapids, Michigan: William B. Eerdmans Publishing Company, 1977, p. 151.

6. Brinkley, p. 31.

7. Brinkley, p. 32.

8. Charles Hyde. "Let's Not Forget the Dodge Brothers," *Michigan History*, March-April 1996, pp. 28–32.

9. Brinkley, p. 66

10. Ibid.

11. May, 1975, p. 274.

12. Brinkley, p. 144.

13. Brinkley, p. 133.

14. Charles Sorenson. *My Forty Years With Ford.* Detroit: Wayne State University Press, 2006, p. 103.

15. May, 1975, p. 191.

16. https://www.autoweek.com/news/a2068111/1909-buick-model-f-driving-david-ds-original-design/

Chapter Four

1. Brinkley, p. 146.

2. Brinkley, p. 161.

3. Brinkley, p. 239.

4. Joseph Cabadas. *River Rouge: Ford's Industrial Colossus.* St. Paul, Minnesota: Motorbooks International, 2004, p. 33.

5. W. N. Hardy. "John F. Dodge Expires in New York of Pneumonia." *Detroit Free Press,* January 15, 1920.

6. Dodge Brothers Motor Cars History (www.dodgemotorcar.com)

7. "Louis Chevrolet" (yourdictionary.com)

8. Ibid.

9. Ibid.

10. Alfred P. Sloan. *My Years With General Motors.* Garden City, New York: Doubleday, 1963, p. 24.

11. Arthur Pound. *The Turning Wheel: The Story of General Motors through Twenty Five Years.* New York: Doubleday, 1934, p. 151.

12. Sloan, p. 32.

13. Brinkely, p. 304.

14. Sloan, p. 267.

15. Sloan, p. 268.

16. Haynes Manual, www.haynes.com

Chapter Five

1. US Bureau of the Census, Historical Statisitcs of the United States; Colonial Times to 1957. Washington, DC: US Government Printing Office, 1960.

2. "How the Great Depression Changed Detroit." *Detroit News,* March 4, 1999.

3. Brinkley, p. 382.

4. Brinkley, p. 419.

5. "The Reminiscences of Mr. Emil Zoerlin." From the Owen W. Bombard interview

series, 1951–1961, p. 233. Accession 65, Benson Ford Research Center.

6. Frank Cormier and William Eaton. *Reuther.* Englewood Cliffs, NJ: Prentice Hall, 1970, p. 98.

7. www.howstuffworks.com/1930-buick-series-40-phaeton.htm

8. Jonathan A . Stein. (ed.). *The Art and Color of General Motors.* Philidephia: Coachbuilt Press, 2008, p. 86.

9. Stein, p. 89.

10. Keith Sword. *The Legend of Henry Ford.* New York: Rienhart and Company, 1945. p. 371.

11. Brinkley, p. 432.

12. Ibid.

Chapter Six

1. Brinkley, p. 453, citing Norman Beasley. *Knudsen: A Biography.* New York: Whittlesey House, 1947, p. 230.

2. Arthur Herman. *Freedom's Forge: How American Business Produced Victory in World War II.* New York: Random House, 2012, pp. 335–337.

3. Brinkley, p. 455.

4. Mira Wilkins and Frank Ernest Hill. *American Business Abroad: Ford on Six Continents.* Detroit: Wayne State University Press, 1964, pp. 316–317.

5. Steve Babson. *Working Detroit.* Detroit: Wayne State University Press, 1986, p. 114.

6. Ed Cray. Chrome *Colossus: General Motors and Its Times.* New York: McGraw Hill Book Company, 1980, p. 318.

7. Ann M. Bos and Randy R. Talbot. "Enough and on Time." (*Michigan History*, March/April 2001), pp. 33–34.

Chapter Seven

1. "Cars of the 1950s: Space Age Fins and Chrome Everything." www.groovyhistory.com/cars-1950s

2. Dunbar, p. 539.

3. Ibid.

4. Mark McCourt. "The Story of Styling: Postwar American Car Designers Are Celebrated in the New Film, 'American Dreaming.'" www.hemmings.com/stories/2014/09/01/the-story-of-styling-postwar-american-car-designers-are-celebrated-in-the-new-film-american-dreaming.

5. Charles Hyde, *Storied Independent Automakers: Nash, Hudson and American Motors.* Detroit: Wayne State University Press, 2009 p. 121.

6. "Whiz Kid Wizardry: Ford Alum Gilmour Says Ford's Postwar Superstars Forged a Proud Legacy of Fiscal Controls, Forward Thinking Management." *Automotive News*, August 16, 1999. www.autonews.com/article/19990816/ANA/908160746/

7. Sloan, p. 263.

8. John Gallagher and Eric Hill, AIA Detroit: *The American Institute of Architects Guide to Detroit Architecture.* Detroit: Wayne State University Press, 2003, p. 321.

9. Stein, p. 90.

10. Thom Taylor. "The Top 10 Reasons Why Packard Died." *Car Profiles*, https://www.hagerty.com/media/car-profiles/10-reasons-why-packard-died/

11. Thomas Sugrue. "Building the Motor Metropolis: Automobiles, Highways and Sprawl." *Automobile in American Life*, http://www.autolife.umd.umich.edu/Race/R_Overview/R_Overview3.htm

Chapter Eight

1. David Halberstam. *The Reckoning.* New York: Open Road Intergrated Media, 1986, p. 7.

2. Charles K. Hyde. *Riding the Roller Coaster: A History of the Chrysler Corporation.* Detroit: Wayne State Univeristy Press, 2003, p. 205.

3. Roger Simpson. "Gas Turbine Car Is Great, but . . ." Detroit Free Press, April 13, 1966.

4. Halberstam, p. 11.

5. Ibid., p. 11

6. Ibid., p. 15.

7. Ibid., p. 18.

8. Murliee Martin. "What About the Malaise Era? More Spcifically, What Abouth This 1979 Ford Granada?" https://www.thetruthaboutcars.com/2011/05/what-about-the-malaise-era-more-specifically-what-about-this-1979-ford-granada/

9. J. Patrick Wright. *On a Clear Day You Can See General Motors.* Grosse Pointe, Michigan: Wright Enterprises, 1979, p. 6.

10. Ralph Nader. *Unsafe At Any Speed.* New York: Grossman Publishers, 1965, p. 211.

11. Wright, p. 53.

12. Lee Iacocca, with William Novak. *Iacocca: A Biography.* New York: Bantam Books, 1984, p. 39.

13. www.mustangspecs.com

14. Iacooca, p. 103.

15. Iacooca, p. 127.

16. Hyde (2003), p. 221.

17. Ibid., pp. 238–240.

18. Ibid., p. 242.

19. Halberstam, p. 340.

20. "Animated Chart of the Day: Market Shares of US Auto Sales, 1961 to 2018." June 28, 2019, www.aei.org/carpe-diem/animated-chart-of-the-day-market-shares-of-us-auto-sales-1961-to-2016/

21. "Foreign Invasion: Imports, Transplants Change Auto Industry Forever." www.wardsauto.com/news-analysis/foreign-invasion-imports-transplants-change-auto-industry-forever

Chapter Nine

1. John W. Wright (ed.). *The New York Times Almanac 2008.* New York: Penguin Books, 2007, p. 415.

2. Bill Vlasic. *Once Upon a Car: The Fall and Resurrection of America's Big Three Automakers—GM, Ford, and Chrysler.* New York: Harper Collins, 2011, p. 13.

3. Chris Isidore. "Big Three Plead for $34B from Congress." https://money.cnn.com/2008/12/04/news/companies/senate_hearing/index.htm

4. Chris Isidore. "GM Made $22.6 Billion. We Lost $10.6 Billion." https://money.cnn.com/2014/05/29/news/companies/gm-profit-bailout/index.html

Epilogue

1. "Is the Chevrolet Volt a True Electric Car? General Motors Defends EV Label." www.mlive.com/auto/2010/10/is_the_chevrolet_volt_a_true_e.html

2. National Motor Vehicle Crash Causation Survey: Report to Congress. https://crashstats.nhtsa.dot.gov/Api/Public/ViewPublication/811059

Sidebars

1. Floyd Clymer. *Treasury of Early American Automobiles 1877–1925.* New York: Bonanza Books, 1950, p. 107.

2. Saturn US Sales Figures. https://carsalesbase.com/us-saturn/

3. James Cobb. "The Return of Detroit's 'Low Priced Three.'" *New York Times,* June 15, 1997.

APPENDIX

BIG THREE CAR MODELS FOR NORTH AMERICA. This is a list of car and truck models manufactured by Detroit's extant major automakers for the US market since the beginning of the industry, along with the years of their production. It does not include models sold exclusively in foreign countries. Note: Production of models overlapping US involvment in World War II (1942–1945) was interrupted for the duration of the conflict.

GENERAL MOTORS

CADILLAC

1909–11 Cadillac Model Thirty
1915–23 Cadillac Type 51
1936–38 Cadillac Series 60
1938–76; 1987–93 Cadillac Sixty Special
1938–51 Cadillac Series 61
1940–64 Cadillac Series 62
1924–30 Cadillac Type V–63
1937–38 Cadillac Series 65
1936–76; 1985–87 Cadillac Series 70
1931–35 Cadillac Series 355
1987–93 Cadillac Allante
2013–19 Cadillac ATS
2016–19 Cadillac ATS–V
1987–92 Cadillac Brougham
2020–present Cadillac CT4

1965–76 Cadillac Calais
1997–2001 Cadillac Catera
2025 Cadillac Celestiq (future)
1982–88 Cadillac Cimarron
1959–2005 Cadillac de Ville
2020–present Cadillac CT5
2016–20 Cadillac CT6
2003–19 Cadillac CTS
1905 Cadillac Model D
2006–11 Cadillac DTS
1952–2002 Cadillac Elderado
2014; 2016 Cadillac ELR
1999–2000; 2002–present Cadillac Escalade
1977–96 Cadillac Fleetwood
1977–86 Cadillac Fleetwood Brougham
2023 Cadillac Lyriq (future)

1903 Cadillac Runabout and Tonneau
1976–2004 Cadillac Seville
2004–16 Cadillac SRX
2005–11 Cadillac STS
1930–37 Cadillac V–12
1930–40 Cadillac V–16
2004–09 Cadillac XLR
2019–present Cadillac XT4
2017–present Cadillac XT5
2020–present Cadillac XT6
2013–19 Cadillac XTS

BUICK

2005–19 Buick LaCrosse
1973–75 Buick Apollo
1936–42; 1954–58; 1973–2005 Buick Century

1903–04 Buick Model B
1905 Buick Model C
1906–10 Buick Models F & G
1910–11 Buick Models 14 & 14B
1971–73 Buick Centurion
1959–90 Buick Electra
2008–present Buick Enclave
2013–present Buick Encore
2020–present Buick Encore GX
2016–present Buick Envision
1970–90 Buick Estate
1973–2004; 2011–20 Buick Regal
1959–63 Buick Invicta
1953–54; 1961–72; 1975–98 Buick Skylark
1959–2005 Buick LaSabre
1931–42 Buick Series 90
1958 Buick Limited

2006–11 Buick Lucerne
1925–28 Buick Master Six
1909–18 Buick Four
1990–2005 Buick Park Avenue
2004–07 Buick Ranier
1988–91 Buick Reatta
1973–2004; 2011–20 Buick Regal
2002–07 Buick Rendezvous
1963–93; 1995–99 Buick Riviera
1936–58; 1991–96 Buick
  Roadmaster
1914–25 Buick Six
1974–80; 1982–89 Buick Skyhawk
1936–58; 1961–69 Buick Special
1964–72 Buick Sport Wagon
1925–28 Buick Standard Six
1930–58 Buick Super
2005–07 Buick Terraza
2012–17 Buick Verano
1963–70 Buick Wildcat

OLDSMOBILE

1938–48 Oldsmobile Series 60
1938–50 Oldsmobile Series 70
1949–99 Oldsmobile 88
1940–96 Oldsmbile 98
1964–80; 1985–87; 1990–91
  Oldsmobile 442
1992–98 Oldsmobile Achieva

1999–2004 Oldsmobile Alero
1995–99; 2001–03 Oldsmobile
  Aurora
1990–94; 1996–2004 Oldsmobile
  Bravada
1901–07 Oldsmobile Curved Dash
1971–92 Oldsmobile Custom
  Cruiser
1961–99 Oldsmobile Cutless
1984–87 Oldsmobile Calais
1988–91 Oldsmobile Cutless Calais
1982–96 Oldsmobile Ciera
1984–96 Oldsmobile Cutless
  Ciera Crusier
1965–97 Oldsmobile Cutless
  Supreme
1982–88 Oldsmobile Firenza
1998–2002 Oldsmobile Intrigue
1964–65 Oldsmobile Jetstar I
1932–38 Oldsmobile L–Series
1916–23 Oldsmobile Light Eight
1910 Oldsmobile Limited
1909–14 Oldsmobile Series 20
1928–38 Oldsmobile F–Series
1923–27 Oldsmobile Model 30
1914 Oldsmobile Model 42
1915–16; 1921–22 Oldsmobile
  Model 43
1907 Oldsmobile Model A

1908 Oldsmobile Model D
1910–11 Oldsmobile Series 22
1912–13 Oldsmobile Series 40
1908 Oldsmobile Model M
1908 Oldsmobile Model X
1906 Oldsmobile Model S
1909 Oldsmobile Model Z
1973–84 Oldsmobile Omega
1990–2004 Oldsmobile Silhouette
1911–12 Oldsmobile Series 28
1913–15; 1917–21 Oldsmobile Six
1960–66; 1974–80 Oldsmobile
  Starfire
1966–92 Oldsmobile Toranado
1989 Oldsmobile Toruing Sedan
1964–77 Oldsmobile Vista Cruiser

PONTIAC

1964–67 Pontiac 2+2
1982–91 Pontiac 6000
1973–77 Pontiac Astre
2000–05 Pontiac Aztek
1958–2005 Pontiac Bonneville
1952–81 Pontiac Catalina
1949–58 Pontiac Chieftain
1969 Pontiac Custom S
1933–42 Pontiac Master
1967–70 Pontiac Executive
1984–88 Pontiac Fiero

1967–2002 Pontiac Firebird
1973–75; 1977–80; 1984–2005
  Pontiac Grand Am
1962–2008 Pontiac Grand Prix
1971–78 Pontiac Grand Safari
1971–75 Pontiac Grand Ville
1959–87 Pontiac Parisienne
1966–71; 2003–06 Pontiac GTO
1962–81 Pontiac LeMans
1954–58 Pontiac Pathfinder
1977–84 Pontiac Phoenix
1955–57; 1958–91; 1987–89
  Pontiac Safari
1926–32; 1935–40 Pontiac Six
1995–2005 Pontiac Sunfire
1960–70; 1987–91 Pontiac Tempest
1939–48 Pontiac Torpedo
2006–09 Pontiac Torrent
1990–99 Pontiac Trans Sport
1960–77 Pontiac Ventura
2003–10 Pontiac Vibe
1997–2009 Pontiac Montana
2006–10 Pontiac Solstice
1954–66 Pontiac Star Chief
1941–51 Pontiac Streamliner
1976–80; 1982–94 Pontiac Sunbird
2005–10 Pontiac G6
2008–09 Pontiac G8

CHEVROLET

1953–57 Chevrolet 150
1953–57 Chevrolet 210
1962–74 Chevrolet 400
1950–81 Chevrolet Bel Air
1941–47 Chevrolet AK Series
1985–2005 Chevrolet Astro
1987–96 Chevrolet Beretta
1958–72 Chevrolet Biscayne
1969–94 Chevrolet K5 Blazer
1983–2005 Chevrolet Blazer/
   GMC Jimmy
1976–86 Chevrolet Chevette
2001–09 Chevrolet Trailblazer
1994–present Chevrolet Tahoe/
   GMC Yukon
2019–present Chevrolet Blazer
2021–present Chevrolet
   Trailblazer
2017–present Chevrolet Bolt
2022 Chevrolet Bolt EUV (future)
1958–61; 1969–75 Chevrolet
   Brookwood
1966–2002; 2010–present
   Chevrolet Camaro
1966–96 Chevrolet Caprice
2006–present Chevrolet Captiva
1982–2005 Chevrolet Cavalier

1982–90 Chevrolet Celebrity
1964–77 Chevrolet Chevelle
1980–85 Chevrolet Citation
2004–09; 2011–present Chevrolet
   Cobalt
1987–91 Chevrolet Corsica
1960–69 Chevrolet Corvair
1953–82; 1984–present Chevrolet
   Corvette
2008–present Chevrolet Cruze
1954–58 Chevrolet Delray
1933 Chevrolet Eagle
1959–60; 1964–87 Chevrolet
   El Camino
2005–present Chevrolet Equinox
1996–present Chevrolet Express
1917 Chevrolet Series F
1941–42 Chevrolet Fleetline
1946–48 Chevrolet Fleetmaster
1964–65 Chevrolet Greenbrier
2006–11 Chevrolet HHR
1958–85; 1994–96; 2000–20
   Chevrolet Impala
1959–60; 1969–72 Chevrolet
   Kingswood
1961–63 Chevrolet Lakewood
1914–15 Chevrolet Light Six
1990–2001 Chevrolet Lumina

1989–96 Chevrolet Lumina APV
1964–83; 1997–present Chevrolet
   Malibu
1969–87; 1994–2007 Chevrolet
   Monte Carlo
1975–80 Chevrolet Monza
1955–61; 1968–72 Chevrolet
   Nomad
1962–79; 1985–88 Chevrolet Chevy
   II/Nova
1959–60 Chevrolet Parkwood
1915–22 Chevrolet Series 490
1927 Chevrolet Series AA Capitol
1928 Chevrolet Series AB National
1929 Chevrolet Series AC
   International
1930 Chevrolet Series AD
   Universal
1931 Chevrolet Series AE
   Independence
1932 Chevrolet Series BA
   Confederate
1911–14 Chevrolet Series C
   Classic Six
1917–18 Chevrolet Series D
1919–22 Chevrolet Series FB
1914–16 Chevrolet Series H
2003–06 Chevrolet SSR

1934–36 Chevrolet Standard
1946–48 Chevrolet Stylemaster
1935–present Chevrolet Suburban
1923–26 Chevrolet Superior
1953–57; 1969–72 Chevrolet
   Townsman
2009–present Chevrolet Traverse
2013–present Chevrolet Trax
2005–08 Chevrolet Uplander
1964–96 Chevrolet/GMC G–Series
   Van
1971–77 Chevrolet Vega
1997–2005 Chevrolet Venture
2011–19 Chevrolet Volt
1958 Chevrolet Yeoman

SATURN

1990–2002 Saturn S–Series
1999–2005 Saturn L–Series
2002–10 Saturn Vue
2003–07 Saturn Ion
2005–07 Saturn Relay
2007–09 Saturn Sky
2007–10 Saturn Outlook
2007–09 Saturn Aura
2008–09 Saturn Astra Ford Cars

FORD

FORD CARS

1896–1901 Ford Quadricycle
1903–04 Ford Model A
1904 Ford Model AC
1904–05 Ford Model C
1905–06 Ford Model F
1906–08 Ford Model K
1906–08 Ford Model N
1907 Ford Model R
1907–09 Ford Model S
1908–27 Ford Model T
1927–31 Ford Model A
1932 Ford Model 18
1932 Ford Model B
1933–34 Ford Model 40
1935 Ford Model 50
1935–36 Ford Model 48
1935–37 Ford CX
1935–37 Ford Model C Ten
1936 Ford Model 67
1937 Ford Model 73/77
1937–38 Ford 7W
1938 Ford Model 81A
1938 Ford Model 82A
1938 Ford Model 92A
1938–61 Ford Prefect

1939 Ford Model 91
1940 Ford Model 01A/02A
1941 Ford Model 11A/1GA
1941–48 Ford Super Deluxe
1942 Ford 2GA
1942 Ford Model 21A/2GA
1946 Ford Model 69A/6GA
1947 Ford Model 74/78
1947 Ford Model 79A/7GA
1948 Ford Model 87HA/89A
1950–51 Ford Crestliner
1950–51 Ford Custom Deluxe
1950–51 Ford Deluxe
1950–91 Ford Country Squire
1952–54 Ford Country Sedan
1952–54 Ford Crestline
1952–56 Ford Customline
1952–99 Ford Ranch Wagon
1955–19; 2002–05 Ford
  Thunderbird
1955–57; 1992–2011 Ford Crown
  Victoria
1955–70 Ford Fairlane
1956 Ford Parklane
1957–58 Ford Del Rio
1957–59 Ford Skyliner
1957–79 Ford Ranchero

1959–74 Ford Galaxie
1960–61 Ford Starliner
1960–70 Ford Falcon
1963 Ford 300
1964–69 Ford GTX1
1964–81 Ford Custom 500
1965–86 Ford LTD
1965–present Ford Mustang
1966–71 Ford Zodiac
1966–72 Ford Executive
1967–70 Ford XL
1968–76 Ford Torino
1968–86 Ford Capri
1970–79 Ford Maverick
1971–80 Ford Pinto
1974–76 Ford Elite
1975–82 Ford Granada
1977–79 Ford LTD II
1978–80; 2011–19 Ford Fiesta
1978–83 Ford Fairmont
1980–81 Ford Durango
1981–2002 Ford Escort
1981–85 Ford Meteor
1982–88 Ford EXP
1983–91 Ford LTD Crown Victoria
1984–94 Ford Tempo
1986–2019 Ford Taurus

1988–92 Ford Festiva
1989–97 Ford Probe
1993–present Ford Mondeo
1994 Ford Aspire
1995–2000 Ford Contour
1998–2003 Ford ZX2
1999–2002 Ford Cougar
2000–19 Ford Focus
2000–09 Ford Focus C–MAX
2003–06 Ford SportKa
2003–06; 2016–present Ford GT
2003–present Ford Everest
2005–07 Ford 500
2005–07 Ford Freestyle
2006–20 Ford Fusion
2006–present Ford S–Max
2012 Ford B–Max
2019–present Ford Puma

FORD VANS

1961–2014 Ford E–Series
1978–2013 Ford Econoline
1995–present Ford Tourneo
2014–present Ford Transit
2009–present Ford Transit
  Connect

FORD MPVS

1986–97 Ford Aerostar
1995–2004 Ford Windstar
1995–present Ford Galaxy
2004–07 Ford Freestar
2007–19 Ford C–MAX

FORD SUVS

1966–96 Ford Bronco
1984–90 Ford Bronco II
1991–present Ford Explorer
1997–present Ford Expidition
2001–present Ford Escape
2000–05 Ford Excursion
2003–present Ford Everest
2004–present Ford Econosport
2005–07 Ford Freestyle
2006–06 Ford Territory
2007–present Ford Edge
2008–09 Ford Taurus X
2008–present Ford Kuga
2009–19 Ford Flex
2020–present Ford Bronco, sixth
  generation

FORD TRUCKS

1925–27 Ford Ford Model TT
1927–31 Ford Model AA
1932–34 Ford Model BB

1932–69 Ford N–Series (heavy
  duty short cab)
1933–34 Ford Model 46
1935 Ford Model 50
1935–36 Ford Model 51
1936 Ford Model 68
1937 Ford Model 75
1937–42; 1946–47 Ford Model 78
1938 Ford Model 81/82
1939–40 Ford Model 91/92/922
1940–42 Ford Model 01/02
1941 Ford Model 19
1941–45 Ford Jeep
1945 Ford Model 59
1945–47 Ford Model 83
1946 Ford Model 69
1946–65 Ford Vanette
1947 Ford Model 79
1948–98 Ford B–Series (bus
  chassis)
1948–present Ford F–Series
1952–60; 1972–82 Ford Courier
1957–79 Ford Ranchero
1957–90 Ford C–Series (medium
  duty truck)
1961–65 Ford H–Series (heavy duty)
1965–81 Ford Explorer Sport Trac
1966 Ford Mustero
1966–96 Ford Bronco (light truck)

1969 Ford Ranchero Rio Grande
1970–98 Ford L–Series
1978–91 Ford CL–Series (heavy
  duty cabover truck)
1981–present Ford Cargo
1983–2012 Ford Ranger
1998–2004 Ford Ranger EV
1999–present Ford Super Duty
2006–present Ford LCF (Low Cab
  Forward)
2018–present Ford Ranger (T6)
1966–77 Ford W–Series

LINCOLN

1920–19 Lincoln Model L
1931–40 Lincoln Model K
1936–42 Lincoln–Zepher
1939–42; 1946–48; 1950–80;
  1982–2002; 2017–20 Lincoln
  Continental
1941–42; 1955 Lincoln Custom
1946–48 Lincoln H–Series
1948–54 Lincoln Cosmopolitan
1949–51 Lincoln EL–Series
1952–59 Lincoln Capri
1955–60 Lincoln Premiere
1977–80 Lincoln Versailles
1981–2011 Lincoln Town Car
2000–06 Lincoln LS
2002 Lincoln Blackwood

2003–06; 2020–present Lincoln
  Aviator
2005–08 Lincoln Mark LT
2006–20 Lincoln MKZ
2009–16 Lincoln MKS
2010–19 Lincoln MKT
2020–present Lincoln Corsair
2016–present Lincoln Nautilus
1998–present Lincoln Navigator

MERCURY

1938–51 Mercury Eight
1949–68 Mercury M–Series
1952–74 Mercury Monterey
1955–56 Mercury Custom
1955–68 Mercury Montclair
1957–91 Mercury Colony Park
1957–68 Mercury Commuter
1945–58 Mercury Turnpike Cruiser
1958–68 Mercury Park Lane
1960–77 Mercury Comet
1962–57 Mercury S–55
1963–2004 Mercury Marauder
1964–71 Mercury Cyclone
1967–2002 Mercury Cougar
1967–86 Mercury Marquis
1968–2007 Mercury Montego
1970–94 Mercury Capri
1974–80 Mercury Bobcat

1975–2011 Mercury Grand
  Marquis
1975–80 Mercury Monarch
1978–83 Mercury Zephyr

1984–94 Mercury Topaz
1986–2009 Mercury Sable
1988–99 Mercury Tracer
1981–87 Mercury Lynx

1982–83 Mercury LN7
1992–2002 Mercury Villager
1995–2000 Mercury Mystique
1997–2010 Mercury Mountaineer

2004–10 Mercury Mariner
2007 Mercury Monterey
2006–11 Mercury Milan

CHRYSLER
(Now part of Stellantis Corporation)

CHRYSLER

2005–present Chrysler 300
2017–present Chrysler Pacifica
1988–present Chrysler Voyager
2011–17 Chrysler 200
1955–65 Chrysler 300 letter series
1999–2004 Chrysler 300M
1962–71; 1979 Chrysler 300 non–
  letter series
1934–37 Chrysler Airflow
1935–37 Chrysler Airstream
1975–80 Chrysler Alpine
2007–09 Chrysler Aspen
1976–79 Chrysler Avenger
1995–2000 Chrysler Cirrus
1993–2004 Chrysler Concorde
1987–89 Chrysler Conquest
1975–83 Chrysler Cordoba
2007–08 Chrysler Crossfire
1983–84 Chrysler E–Class

1983–86 Chrysler Executive
1984–89 Chrysler Fifth Avenue
1976–77 Chrysler Galant
1926–54; 1990–93 Chrysler
  Imperial (from 1955–83 Imperial
  existed as separate division of
  Chrysler Corporation)
1952 Chrysler Imperial Parade
  Phaeton
1984–86 Chrysler Laser
1977–95 Chrysler LeBaron
1994–97; 1999–2001 Chrysler LHS
1940–41; 1950; 1961–81 Chrysler
  Newport
1939–96 Chrysler New Yorker
1983; 1990–93 Chrysler New Yorker
  Fifth Avenue
2004–08 Chrysler Pacifica
2001–02 Chrysler Prowler
2001–10 Chrysler PT Cruiser
1937–42; 1946–50 Chrysler Royal

1939–53; 1957–60; 1961–66
  Chrysler Saratorga
1995–2010 Chrysler Sebring
1989–91 Chrysler TC by Maserati
1926 Chrysler Touring
1941–77; 1990–2016 Chrysler
  Town and Country
2000–03 Chrysler Voyager/Grand
  Voyager
1940–61 Chrysler Windsor

DODGE

1970–74; 1977–83; 2008–present
  Dodge Challenger
1966–78; 1982–87; 2006–present
  Dodge Charger
1963–64 Dodge 330
1982–83 Dodge 400
1963–64 Dodge 440
1983–88 Dodge 600
1962–65 Dodge Custom 880

1981–89 Dodge Aries
1976–80 Dodge Aspen
1995–2000; 2008–14 Dodge
  Avenger
2007–12 Dodge Caliber
1971–94 Dodge Colt
1984–86 Dodge Conquest
1949–59; 1965–76 Dodge Coronet
1946–48 Dodge Custom
1955–59 Dodge Custom Royal
1960–76 Dodge Dart
1984–93 Dodge Daytona
1946–48 Dodge Deluxe
1977–89 Dodge Diplomat
1988–93 Dodge Dynasty
1930–33 Dodge Eight
1927–38 Dodge Fast Four
1993–2004 Dodge Intrepid
1960–62; 1985–89 Dodge Lancer
1978–89; 2005–08 Dodge Magnum
1960 Dodge Matador

1949–54 Dodge Meadowbrook

1980–83 Dodge Mirada

1914–22 Dodge Model 30

1965–78; 1990–92 Dodge Monaco

1994–2005 Dodge Neon

1978–90 Dodge Omni

1960–73 Dodge Polara

1987–89 Dodge Raider

1954–59 Dodge Royal

1927–30 Dodge Senior

1923–25 Dodge Series 116

1987–94 Dodge Shadow

1957–59 Dodge Sierra

1929–49 Dodge Six

1989–95 Dodge Spirit

1928–29 Dodge Standard

1991–96 Dodge Stealth

1995–2006 Dodge Stratus

1979–81 Dodge St. Regis

1928–29 Dodge Victory

1992–2017 Dodge Viper

1949–52 Dodge Wayfarer

PLYMOUTH

1946–50 Plymouth De Luxe

1949–61 Plymouth Suburban

1951–53 Plymouth Cambridge

1951–52 Plymouth Concord

1951–53 Plymouth Cranbrook

1954–70 Plymouth Belvedere

1954–58 Plymouth Plaza

1954–64 Plymouth Savoy

1956–78 Plymouth Fury

1960–76 Plymouth Valiant

1964–74 Plymouth Barracuda

1965–74 Plymouth Satellite

1966–71 Plymouth GTX

1968–80 Plymouth Roadrunner

1970–76 Plymouth Duster

1970 Plymouth Superbird

1970–73 Plymouth Cricket

1974–81 Plymouth Trail Duster

1974–2000 Plymouth Voyager/
  Grand Voyager

1975–89 Plymouth Gran Fury

1976–80 Plymouth Volare

1976–80 Plymouth Arrow

1978–90 Plymouth Horizon

1978–83 Plymouth Sapporo

1979–82 Plymouth Arrow Truck

1979–82 Plymouth Champ

1981–89 Plymouth Reliant

1983–88 Plymouth Caravelle

1983–87 Plymouth Turismo

1984–94 Plymouth Colt Vista

1984–86 Plymouth Conquest

1987–94 Plymouth Sundance

1989–95 Plymouth Acclaim

1990–94 Plymouth Laser

1994–2001 Plymouth Neon

1996–2000 Plymouth Breeze

1997–2001 Plymouth Prowler

DESOTO

1929–32 DeSoto Series K–SA

1933–34 DeSoto Series SC–SD

1934–36 DeSoto Airflow

1935–36 DeSoto Airstream

1937–42 DeSoto Series S

1946–52 DeSoto Custom

1946–52 DeSoto Deluxe

1946–61 DeSoto Diplomat

1952–59 DeSoto Firedome

1953–54 DeSoto Powermaster

1955–60 DeSoto FireFlite

1956–60 DeSoto Adverturer

1957–59 DeSoto Firesweep

INDEX

1932 Hunger March, 58
1933 Chicago World's Fair, 67
1937 Sit-Down Strike, 60, 63, 69
9/11 Attacks, 116
AFL/CIO, See *American Federation of Labor*.
African-American/Black, 69, 98, 120
ALAM, See *Association of Licensed Automobile Manufacturers*.
Alfa Romeo, 95
Alger, Russell, Jr., 26
American Bantam Company, 79
American Dreaming, 84
American Federation of Labor, 74
American Motors Corporation, 88, 96, 143
Anderson Electric Car Company, See *Detroit Electric Company/ Detroit Electric*.
Anderson, John W., 30
Arkus-Duntov, Zora, 95
Armstrong, Louis, 149
Association of Licensed Automobile Manufacturers, 32
Aston Martin, 113
automated vehicles, 132
B-24 Liberator Bomber, 76–77, 80, 98, 143
Baruch, Bernard, 72
Begley, Ed, Jr., 126
Bendix Aviation, 89
Bennett, Charles, 30
Bennett, Harry, 62–63, 69, 80
Benz & Companie Rheinische Gasmotoren-Fabrik, 9
Benz, Karl, 9
Bertoia, Harry, 90
Big Three, 10, 57, 60, 71, 74, 83–84, 98, 101, 104, 106, 113, 115–118, 143, 155

Blitzkrieg, 72, 78
Bloomfield, G.T., 19
"Bomber Road", See *Detroit Industrial Freeway*.
Bosworth, Charles, 89
Bourdain, Anthony, x
Bowen, Lem, 24
Brayton, George, 32
Breech, Ernest, 89
Breer, Carl, 49
Briggs Manufacturing Company, 60, 96
Briggs, Walter, 60
Brinkley, Douglas, 4, 16, 34
Britain/British, 8, 72, 79
Buick Auto-Vim Company, 36
Buick/Buick Motor Company, 36–37, 45–46, 49, 60, 64, 68, 92, 136, 141, 144, 155–156
Buick David Dunbar, 36
Bush, George W., 118
Cadillac, Antoine de la Mothe, 24
Cadillac/Cadillac Automobile Company, 24–25, 32, 45, 50, 52, 67–68, 83, 92, 96, 144–145, 155
Calder, Alexander, 90
Cartercar, 45
Carter, Jimmy, 106, 111
Cavelier, Robert, 145
Centennial Exhibition, 32
Chalmers, Hugh, 134–135
Chalmers Motor Company, 49, 110, 134–135, 148
Chapin, Roy, 88, 134–135
Chevrolet, 46, 48, 53, 59, 68, 72, 83, 92, 95, 101, 104, 107, 110, 114, 128, 136, 144–145, 148
Chevrolet Bolt, 127–128
Chevrolet Camaro, 101

Chevrolet Corvair, 107
Chevrolet Corvette, 83, 94–95, 114, 143
Chevrolet, Louis, 46, 48
Chevrolet Motor Car Company. See *Chevrolet*.
Chevrolet Vega, 104, 110
Chevrolet Volt, 127–128
Chevy, See *Chevrolet*.
Chrysler Airflow, 64
Chrysler Building, 65
Chrysler Corporation, 49, 57, 64–65, 69, 78, 83–84, 96, 98, 101–103, 110–111, 113, 116–118, 135, 143–144, 148, 150, 160
Chrysler Imperial, 148
Chrysler Loan Guarantee Act, 111
Chrysler Newport, 110
Chrysler Sebring, 144
Chrysler Turbine, 102–103
Chrysler, Walter, 36, 49, 110, 135, 148
CIO, See *Congress of Industrial Organizations*.
Civil War, 1
Clark and Son, 12
Clooney, Rosemary, 149
Coffin, Howard, 134
Communism, 58, 60
Congress of Industrial Organizations, 74
Consolidated Aircraft Company, 76
Cooley, Eugene, 20
Cord, 57
Couzens, James, 30
Cuba/Cuban, 68
Cugnot, Nicolas, 8
Curtis, Frank, 8
Cyrus Lawrence, 104
Daimler-Benz, 9, 113
Daimler, Gottlieb, 9, 15
Daimler Motoren-Gesellschaft, 9

Da Vinci, Leonardo, 8
Davis, David, 106
Davis, William, 1
Dayton Engineering Laboratories, See *Delco*.
Dearborn, 12, 16–17, 39, 42, 58–59, 62
Delco, 48
DeLorean, John, 107–108, 146
Deming, W. Edwards, 112
Democratic Party, 60
Denby, Edwin, 136
Denmark/Danish, 72
DeSoto, 49, 135, 148
DeSoto Firedome, 148
DeSoto FireFlite, 148
DeSoto Firesweep, 148
de Soto, Hernando, 148
Detroit Arsenal Tank Plant, 78
Detroit Automobile Company, 22
Detroit Auto Show, 94
Detroit Car and Manufacturing Company, 3
Detroit Car Wheel Company, 3
Detroit Cultural Center, 57
Detroit Dry Dock Company, 3
Detroit Electric Company/Detroit Electric, 32, 126, 140–141
Detroit Free Press, 44, 58, 104
Detroit Illuminating Company, 22
Detroit Industrial Freeway, 98
Detroit Institute of Arts, xi
Detroit Institute of Automotive Styling, 92
Detroit News, 20, 63
Detroit Police Department, 136
Detroit Public Library, xi, 18
Detroit River, 2, 42
Detroit Shipbuilding Company, 3
Detroit Stove Works, 3

Detroit Symphony Orchestra, xi
Detroit Unemployment Council, 58
Detroit-Windsor Tunnel, 57
Deutz-AG-Gasmotorengabrik, 9
Dillon, Read & Company, 44, 49
Dodge Challenger, 101
Dodge/Dodge Brothers Motor Car Company, 32, 34, 41, 44, 49, 86, 101, 110–111, 135, 148, 160–161
Dodge, John and Horace, 28–30, 34, 39, 41, 44
Dodge, Matilda and Anna, 44, 49
Dodge Model 30–35, 41
Dodge Omni, 110
Dort, J. Dallas, 36
Drake, J. Walter, 136
Durant, William, 21, 24, 36, 45–46, 48–49, 145
Duryea, Charles, 10, 11
Duryea, Frank, 10
Duryea Motor Wagon Company, 10
Duryea Power Company, 10
Earl, Harley, 52, 84, 90, 92, 95, 145
Eblinger, Wilhelm, 9
Edison Illuminating Company, 17
Edison, Thomas, 59
Edsel, See *Ford Edsel (car)*.
Edsel Show, The, 149
electric cars, 8, 19, 32, 102, 125–128, 130, 140–141
Elmore, 44
End of Detroit, The, 120
Engel, Elwood, 103
England/English, 7–8, 12, 126
Ewing, 44
Exner, Virgil, 84
Fiat SpA, 46, 113, 118
Fisher Body Division, 52, 60
Fisher Building, 57

Fisher Freeway, 99
Fisher, Lawrence, 52
Flint Road Cart Company, 36
Flocken, Andreas, 126
Ford Airstream, 130
Ford Cabriolet, 59,
Ford, Clara, 16, 50, 62, 69, 141
Ford Edsel (car), 149
Ford, Edsel (person), 50, 54, 62, 69, 72, 76, 80, 150
Ford Engineering Laboratory, 59
Ford, Henry, xi, 4, 8, 12, 15–17, 20, 22–23, 30, 32–34, 39–42, 44–46, 50, 58, 62, 69, 72–73, 80, 82, 120, 134, 141
Ford, Henry, II, 89, 109
Fordism, 40
Ford Maverick, 110
Ford Model 18, 59
Ford Model A, 30, 33, 42, 53–55, 59
Ford Model B, 33, 53
Ford models AC, C, F, K, N, R, S, 33, 36, 53
Ford Model T, 32–34, 41–42, 48, 53, 145
Ford Motor Company/Ford, 30–32, 35, 38–42, 44, 50, 53, 57–60, 62–63, 67, 69, 72–73, 76, 79–80, 82, 95, 98, 101, 103, 108–111, 113, 116–118, 125, 127, 130–131, 136, 143, 148–150, 158
Ford Museum of American Innovation, 17
Ford Mustang, 101, 108–109, 127, 144
Ford Mustang Mach-E, 127
Ford Pinto, 104
Ford Service Department, 58, 62–63
Ford Thunderbird, 95
Ford Whiz Kids, 89
Ford, William, 16
France/French, 8–9, 46, 72, 74, 78, 89, 120, 145
Frankensteen, Richard, 63
Franklin, 57
Frazer, Joseph W., 143
Freer, Charles Lang, 3

Frigidaire, 92, 94
Frontenac Motor Car Company, 46
Fry, Vernon, 30
Galamb, Joseph, 33
General Motors Building, 48, 107
General Motors Caravan of Progress, 67–68, 94
General Motors/GM, 21, 24, 45, 48–49, 52, 57, 59–60, 62, 67, 69, 72, 75, 84–85, 88, 90, 92–93, 95–96, 101, 107–108, 113, 115–118, 123, 126, 128, 144–148, 150, 155
General Motors Parade of Progress, See General Motors Caravan of Progress.
General Motors Technical Center, 90–92
Germany/German, 9, 72, 78, 92, 116, 126
Gettelfinger, Ron, 118
GI Bill, 84
Gilmour, Allan, 89
Glennie, Ruth, 92
GM, See General Motors/GM.
GMC, 45, 157
GM EV-1, 126, 128
GM Heritage Center, 75
GM Motorama, 68, 94–95
GM Styling Dome, 90, 92
Goldman Sachs, 118
Graham-Paige Motor Company, 136, 143
Gravel, Benjamin, 141
Gray, John, 30
Great Britain, See Britain/British.
Great Depression, 57–58, 63–64, 67, 80, 83, 136, 138, 148
Great Recession, 117
Gulf of Mexico, 145
Gurney, Sir Goldsworthy, 8
Halberstam, David, 106, 112
Hanks, Tom, 126
Hastings, Charles, 136
Haynes, Frederick, 44
Hecker, Frank, 3
Henry Ford Company, 22, 24
Highland Park Ford Plant, 34–35, 38, 40, 42

Honda, 109, 112–113
Hope, Bob, 149
Horton, Peter, 126
Hudson, Joseph Lowthian, 88, 96, 135, 148
Hudson Motors, 88
Huebner, George, 102
Hummer, 123
Hupp Motor Car Company, 32, 136
Hupp, Robert "Bobby", 136
Hyatt Roller Bearing Company, 48
hybrids, 67, 125, 127–128
Hyde, Charles, 110
hydrogen fuel cells, 130
Hyundai, 113
Iacocca, Lee, 100, 108–109, 111, 148
Interstate Highway System, 98
Iraq/Iraqi, 115
Ireland/Irish, 16
Italy/Italian, 108, 118, 146
Jaguar, 95, 113
Japan/Japanese, 74, 112–113, 128
Jeep, 79, 143
John R. Keim Company, 39
Joy, Henry Bourne, 18, 26
Kahn, Albert, 26, 34, 78
Kaiser-Frazer, 143
Kaiser, Henry J., 143
Kaiser Motors/Kaiser-Jeep/Kaiser-Willys, See Kaiser-Frazer.
Kaiser Permanente, 143
K-Car, See Plymouth Reliant.
Keating, Thomas, 95
Keller, K.T., 78
Kelvinator Company, See Nash-Kelvinator.
Kettering, Charles, 67
Kia, 113
Kilpatrick, James R., 63
King, Charles, xi, 4, 15, 20
King Motor Car Company, 15
Klug, Thomas, 3
Knudsen, William S., 39, 72–73, 75–76, 78

Korea/Korean, 113
Korean War, 88, 94
Kraus, Henry, 60
Kuwait/Kuwaiti, 115
Laird, Ray, 59
Land Rover, 113
La Salle, 52, 145
Lawson, George, 86
Lehigh University, 108
Leland, Henry, 24, 36, 50
Leland, Wilfred, 50
Lend-Lease Act, 72, 79
Leno, Jay, 103
Library of Congress, vi, viii, xi, 2, 4, 6, 9–12, 24–26, 28–29, 33, 40, 42, 45–46, 48–51, 55, 60, 65, 68, 70, 72–76, 78–79, 88, 90–91, 107, 116, 123, 135, 139–141, 149
Lincoln/Lincoln Motor Company, 50–51, 67, 150
Lincoln Mercury Division, 89, 149–150
Linder, Jennette, 92
Loewy, Raymond, 136
Longyear, Sandra, 92
Low Countries, 72, 78
Lundy, J. Edward, 89
Macauley, Alvin, 73
Malaise Era, 106
Malcolmson, Alexander, 30
Manufacturer's Challenge Cup, 22, 30
Marquette, 64, 145
Marr, Walter, 36
Marshall, George, 79
Martin, Murilee, 106
Mason, George W., 88, 96
Maxwell-Chalmers. See Chalmers Motor Company.
Maxwell, Charley, 104
Maxwell Motors. See Chalmers Motor Company.
Maybach, Wilhelm, 9
May, George, 20
Maynard, Micheline, 120
McCoy, Elijah, 1

McNamara, Robert, 89
Mercury, See Lincoln Mercury Division.
Mercury Cougar, 150
Mercury Cyclone, 150
Mercury Mariner, 150
Mercury Montego, 150
Mercury Mountaineer, 150
Mercury Villager, 150
Mexico/Mexican, 68
MG, 95
Michigan Car Company, 3, 15
Michigan Central Station, 124–125
Michigan National Guard, 60
Michigan State Fairgrounds, 3
Michigan Stove Company, 3
Michigan Supreme Court, 41
Miller, Arjay, 89
Mitchell, Bill, 92
Mississippi River, 145
Model A, See Ford Model A.
Model T, See Ford Model T.
Morrison, William, 8
Mortimer, Wyndham, 60
Mulally, Alan, 118
Murphy, Frank, 60
Murphy, William, 24
Nader, Ralph, 107
Nance, James, 96
Nardelli, Robert, 118
Nash, Charles, 88
Nash-Kelvinator, 67, 88, 96
Nash Motors, See Nash-Kelvinator.
Nash Rambler, 88
National Cash Register, 134
National Highway Traffic Safety Administration, 107, 132
National Labor Relations Act, See Wagner Act.
Nazi, 72–73, 78
Newberry, Truman, 26
New Deal, 58
New Departure Manufacturing Company, 48

Newsweek, 109
New York World's Fair, 109
Nissan, 112
Northern Manufacturing Company, 15
Norway/Norwegian, 72
Oakland/Oakland Motor Car
    Company, 32, 45, 98, 145–146
Oil Crisis, 101, 104, 106, 110
Oldfield, Barney, 22–23
Olds Curved Dash, 20–21, 146
Olds Gasoline Engine Company, 20
Oldsmobile, 45, 52, 60, 68, 92, 145–146,
    148–149, 156
Oldsmobile Alero, 146
Olds Motor Vehicle Company, 20
Olds Motor Works, 12, 21, 24, 34, 136,
    138, 144
Olds, Pliny, 12
Olds, Ransom, xi, 4, 12, 20–21, 28, 88,
    138, 144, 146
Olds, Wallace, 12
*On a Clear Day You Can See General
    Motors*, 107
OPEC, 104
Organization of Petroleum Exporting
    Countries, See *OPEC*.
Otto, Nicolaus August, 9
Packard, 18, 26–27, 32, 72–73, 88, 96
Packard, James Ward and
    William Dowd, 26
Parker, Thomas, 8, 126
Pearl Harbor, 74, 78
Peerless, 57
Peninsular Car Company, 3
Penske, Roger, 147
P.F. Olds and Son, 12
Pierce-Arrow, 57

Piquette Plant, 32–34, 40
Plymouth, 49, 110, 135, 148
Plymouth Cordage Company, 148
Plymouth Horizon, 110
Plymouth Reliant, 100, 148
Plymouth Voyager, 148
Pohlmann, Marjorie Ford, 92
Pontiac, 32, 45, 60, 68, 84, 92, 101,
    107–108, 145–146
Pontiac Bonneville, 146
Pontiac Firebird, 146
Pontiac G6, 146
Pontiac Grand Prix, 146
Pontiac GTO, 101, 108, 146
Pope-Hartford, 19
Pratt Institute, 92
Princeton University, 108
Probst, Karl, 79
Project Opel, 95
Pullman, George, 3
Rackham, Horace, 30
Read, Nathan, 8
Reith, Francis, 89
Remy Electric, 48
R.E. Olds Motor Car Company, See
    REO Motor Car Company.
REO Model B Runabout, 138, 144
REO Motor Car Company, 138, 144
REO Speed Wagon, 138
Reuther, Roy, 60
Reuther, Walter, 60, 62–63
Ribicoff, Abraham, 107
Riccardo, John, 110–111
Riding the Roller Coaster, 110
Rochas, Alphonse Beau de, 9
Roche, James, 107
Roche, Kevin, 90

Rolls-Royce, 72–73
Romney, George, 88, 96
Roosevelt, Franklin, 72, 74, 78
Rose, Max, 9
Rother, Helene, 92
Rouge Complex, 41–42, 58, 62–63, 69, 79
Russel, George B., 3
Russel Wheel and Foundry
    Company, 3, 15
Saab, 113, 123
Saarinen, Eero, 90
St. John Craig, 2
Salustro, Greg, 84
Saturn, 123, 147
Sauer, Peggy, 92
Schultz, Carl, 59
Scientific American, 12
Scott, Richard H., 138
Second Industrial Revolution, 3, 120
Security and Exchange Commission, 86
Selden, George/Selden Patent, 32
Service Department, See *Ford Service
    Department*.
Skelton, Owen, 49
Sloan, Alfred P., 36, 48, 52, 72, 90, 94
Smith, Roger, 147
Smith, Samuel L. and Fred, 20–21, 45,
    138, 144
Sorenson, Charles, 35
Spain/Spanish, 148
Spanish Flu, 44
Sparrow, Edward W., 20
Stanley Steamer, 8
Stebbins, Arthur C., 20
Stevens-Duryea, 10
Stevens, Joshua, 10
Stimson, Henry, 76

Strelow, Albert, 30
Strengell, Marianne, 90
Studebaker, 49, 88, 96–97
Studebaker-Packard, See *Studebaker*.
Stutz, 57
Sugrue, Thomas, 98
Sweden/Swedish, 113
TARP, 118
Thomas B. Jeffery Company, 88
Thomas-Detroit, 134
Thornton, Charles "Tex", 89
Townsend, Lynn, 110
Toyota, 116, 128
Toyota Prius, 128
Tremulis, Alex, 86
Troubled Asset Relief Program,
    See *TARP*.
Tucker Corporation, 86
Tucker, Preston, 86
UAW, See *United Auto Workers*.
Unemployed Councils of the USA, 58
unions, 40, 58, 60, 62–63, 69, 71, 74, 80
United Auto Workers, 60, 62–63, 69, 74,
    111, 116–118
United Motors Corporation, 48
United States Air Force/Corps 24, 73, 89
United States Army, 24, 73, 76, 78–79, 89
United States Congress, 60, 74, 111,
    118, 132
United States Department of
Transportation, 107
United States Navy, 42, 75, 95
United States Senate, 107, 118
United States Supreme Court, 69
Unsafe at Any Speed, 107
V8 engine, 59, 83, 95, 145–146, 150
Vanderbilt, Suzanne, 92

Viking, 145
Volkswagen, 65, 113
Volo Auto Museum, 32, 54, 108, 114
Voluntary Employees Beneficiary
    Association, 117
Volvo, 65, 113
Wagner Act, 60, 69
Wagoner, Rick, 118
Wall Street, 62, 94, 104
Walter P. Reuther Library, ix, 15, 20, 23,
    34, 36, 53, 56, 62–63, 67, 75, 77, 80,
    82, 96, 99, 106, 108, 111, 143
War Production Board, 70
Warren Motor Car, 50
Warren Tank Plant, 78
Westinghouse, 16
Whiting, William, 36
Who Killed the Electric Car?, 126
Willow Run Plant, 76–78, 98, 143
Willys-Overland Company, 49, 79, 135,
    143
Winton, Alexander, 22, 26, 32
Winton Motor Carriage Company,
    26, 32
Wolverton and Company, 3
women, 92, 108
Woodall, Charles, 30
World Columbian Exposition, 3,
    12, 15
World War I, 42, 79, 135
World War II, xi, 68, 71, 74, 78, 84, 86,
    90, 96, 98, 102, 112, 120, 143, 148,
    150, 155
Yom Kippur War, 104
Zeder, Fred, 49